Around The World in 80 Meals
The Best of Cruise Ship Cuisine

Diana Rubino

TABLE OF CONTENTS

INTRODUCTION
The History of Cruising

The history of pleasure cruises spans about 50 years, but in the early 20th century, passengers needing to cross the Atlantic travel on the only vessels available, mail ships. With decades of upgrades they became ocean liners, the most famous being Lusitania, Titanic, and the first Queen Mary. Today, the competitiveness of the cruise industry demands that cruise lines top each other with larger, taller, grander luxury ships with amenities found in the most luxurious resorts. Far from being a means to an end, the crowded, treacherous, often dangerous ocean crossing in a mail ship's hold, cruising today is the ultimate in luxury with staterooms rivaling 5-star hotels and cuisine matching the world's top restaurants.

The first Transatlantic cruise took place in 1840 on a Cunard mail steamship. These ships crossed the ocean faster than older vessels. Eventually passengers became more demanding of their fare, and amenities included a cow providing fresh milk.

The first vessel built strictly for cruising, a yacht named for Kaiser Wilhelm II's daughter, the Prinzessin Victoria Luise, had her maiden voyage 1900 from Germany to the Mediterranean. She had first class cabins, a library and darkroom. It ran aground six years later.

By the early 20th century, cruise lines such as White Star and Cunard competed fiercely for rich passengers who could afford the rising costs of an Atlantic crossing and were used to being served in style. In 1912 Titanic was the first true luxury liner. Her maiden voyage from Southampton, England was her last. She and comparable ships such as the Mauritania and Lusitania boasted luxurious cabins with hot running water in first class, fine dining and entertainment, and strict barriers between the classes.

The Lusitania

Passenger jets began crossing the Atlantic in the 1950s, and the cruise industry suffered accordingly. Jetting replaced cruising as a means to cross the ocean, so cruise lines sent their ships to the Caribbean, opening a new market, cruising the islands as a vacation in itself.

With all these ships cruising the islands, by the mid-60s, a Caribbean getaway was within the reach of more travelers. In 1965, Princess was the first line to offer an affordable itinerary on the Princess Pat, sailing from California down the Mexican coastline. The following year saw the birth of Norwegian Cruise Line (NCL) whose ships contained affordable cabins for budget-conscious travelers. Royal Caribbean Cruise Line followed in 1970, and in 1972 Carnival's "Fun Ships" gobbled up many existing lines such as Cunard, Holland America, and Seabourn. Today, cruising can accommodate any budget large or small, and over 200 cruise ships circle the globe, with several more in the making, always grander, offering more, making the cruising experience second to none.

A huge part of the cruising experience is the cuisine. Gourmet chefs prepare lavish onboard meals, and kitchens are open 24 hours a day for passengers' dining pleasure. The early luxury liners offered menus that rivaled the world's top restaurants, and they still do.

Browse this 1907 menu from Cunard's RMS Mauretania.

At the time this represented the finest cuisine that ships had

to offer. This book contains menus from today's cruise lines,

offering a huge variety of appetizers, soups, salads, entrees

and desserts, featuring healthy low-fat and sugar-free

alternatives. Cruising has come a long way in the last 100+

years, and menus have expanded on the same scale as the

ships themselves!

CHAPTER ONE

Embarkation – *Queen Mary 2*

In times gone by, before jumbo jets and mass transit,

travel was leisurely. Trains and ocean liners were the primary

sources of long-distance travel, and catered to the well-

heeled, with opulent compartments, dining cars, staterooms,

and restaurants. An ocean voyage was the highlight of the

'grand tour of Europe' and the ships were as sophisticated

and elegant as any European capital. Naturally, the first choice for a transatlantic carrier was the Cunard Line.

Cunard's fleet of ocean liners was the world's grandest, affording passengers all the luxury and comfort of a five-star Paris, Rome, or Vienna hotel. Rivaling royal palaces in grandeur and sumptuousness, Cunard liners transported wealthy robber barons and moguls as well as world leaders and movie stars, who wined and dined in the elegant restaurants and strolled the promenade decks in tie and tails, evening gowns, and glittering jewels.

Now modern travelers can re-live this opulent era on Cunard's Flagship Queen Mary 2, and like our forebears, enjoy the same luxury and splendor that made the journey transcend the destination. Queen Mary 2 had her maiden voyage from Southampton, England in April 2004 and emerged out of the mist in New York Harbor just before 8 a.m. six days later. Queen Mary 2 is reminiscent of the grand ocean liners of old, including her predecessor the Queen

Mary, which was retired in 1967 and is now docked in Long Beach, California. Queen Mary 2 is four football fields long, and is three times the size of the Titanic.

You just don't spend $800 million on a ship and leave it to chance that dining will be anything short of stellar. Cunard stacked the deck on Queen Mary 2, decorating her dining rooms in the tradition of the ocean liners of times gone by, whose restaurants rivaled New York's early 20th century "lobster palaces" such as Rector's and Murray's Roman Gardens. These lobster palaces, with grand staircases and Louis XIV furnishings illuminated in thousands of electric lights and reflected in floor-to-ceiling mirrors, made the millionaire patrons feel like royalty in the court of Louis XIV, as period-costumed waiters in ruffled shirts and silk stockings brought their sumptuous meals to their linen-covered tables graced with crystal and genuine silverware. The 3-story Brittania Restaurant, Queen Mary 2's main dining room, most closely resembles Gilded Age dining salons and lobster palaces.

Cunard also enlisted heralded New York chef Daniel Boulud to be the ship's culinary adviser and celebrity chef Todd English to create his own 156-seat, Mediterranean-style restaurant on board. As a Cunard ship, Queen Mary 2 has a grand dining tradition to live up to. The dining experience on Queen Mary 2 is the main attraction of the voyage. Waiters trained in the fine art of Cunard White Star Service serve culinary delights created by a team of experienced chefs in the ten restaurants. The menus have been greatly expanded since the old Queen Mary made her voyages, offering a wide range of delicious selections to please every palate, and the largest wine selection on the seven seas.

And so our virtual fantasy cruise begins as the world-famous Queen Mary 2 commences her maiden transatlantic crossing. You leave London's Waterloo station and enjoy a scenic train ride through the lush English countryside.

Transferring at Southampton you can only gape in astonishment at your first glimpse of this magnificent vessel. You haven't felt this awestruck since your first breathtaking view of Egypt's pyramids. Formalities over, you settle into your sumptuous stateroom, catch your breath and then eagerly explore from prow to stern. As you reach the top decks you feel the faintest thrumming of high powered engines beneath your feet and the ship begins to move. You peer down at the distant passersby as they wave and cheer you off.

After leaving its home port of Southampton Queen Mary 2 steams majestically through the Solent, past the Isle of Wight, and into the English Channel heading for the Atlantic Ocean. That evening finds you sitting in the Britannia restaurant. A white gloved waiter hands you a glorious full color menu that you'll treasure as a collector's item for years to come.......

QUEEN MARY 2

For over three decades Queen Elizabeth 2 ruled the North Atlantic, continuing the tradition of her forbears Queen Mary and Queen Elizabeth.

In May 1998, when Cunard Line was purchased by Carnival Corporation, one of the first projects was to investigate the design and development for a new class of superliner – the first to be designed since QE2 – codenamed 'Project Queen Mary'.

On 6 November 2000 a formal contract was signed with the French shipyard Chantiers de l'Atlantique for Queen Mary 2 – the largest (151,400-tons), longest (1,132 feet / 345 metres), tallest (236 feet / 72 metres), widest (135 feet / 41 metres) and most expensive (£550 million / $800 million) passenger ship ever built.

Queen Mary 2 entered service on 12 January 2004 after being named by Her Majesty Queen Elizabeth II, at what was the most spectacular naming ceremony ever, four days earlier.

Everything about Queen Mary 2 is superlative and she offers a host of 'firsts' and exclusives. 79% of cabins feature private balconies. There is artwork worth over £3.5 million (US $5 million) on board. The world's first floating Planetarium offers virtual reality rides through the galaxies. A cultural academy is operated by the University of Oxford. She offers the first suites with private lift access, the first Canyon Ranch Spa at sea, the first Veuve Clicquot Champagne Bar at sea, the largest Library at sea (with 8,000 hardbacks, 500 paperbacks, 200 audio books and 100 CD Roms, the largest ballroom with the largest dancefloor at sea, workshops and master classes performed by RADA (the Royal Academy of Dramatic Arts), the longest jogging track at sea and the largest and most extensive wine cellar at sea.

And if that's not enough, the 'Queen Mary 2' illuminated signs below the funnel are the largest illuminated ship's name signs in maritime history!

Queen Mary 2, 2004

THE GRANDEST OCEAN LINER EVER BUILT

2002

16 January
Pamela Conover, Cunard's President, presses the button to cut the first sheet of steel for Queen Mary 2.

March Update
- 73% of steel material ordered
- 2 panels (out of 580) completed
- 6% of the steel cut

11 June
Cunard announces Maiden Voyage date (12 January 2004) and 2004 schedule for new flagship.

June Update
- 94% of steel material ordered
- 62 panels (out of 580) completed
- 28% of the steel cut (9,700 tons)

4 July
Keel Laying Ceremony takes place

8 - 11 August
First block of Queen Mary 2 floats for the first time and moves into the second position of the building dock.

September Update
- 273 panels (out of 580) completed
- 70% of the steel cut (23,500 tons)
- 14 blocks (out of 97) are on board

1 December
Queen Mary 2 floats down to the deeper end of the dry dock.

Grand Lobby under construction

2003

January Update
- 620 panels (out of 620) completed
- 100% of the steel cut (33,700 tons)
- 94 blocks (out of 100) are on board

5 February
450 crew cabins and 8 balcony cabins have been loaded by this date. About 87% of cabin windows and portholes are installed.

16 March
Mast Stepping Ceremony takes place

21 March
Queen Mary 2 leaves the building dock for the first time and is moved to the fitting out basin.

May Update
- Approximately 1,000 of the 2,017 passenger and crew cabins have been installed.
- Installation of funnel and mast completed.

June
The painting of Queen Mary 2's exterior begins. Installation of the four 'pods' completed.

25 - 29 September
Queen Mary 2 takes to the open sea for the first time and undergoes her first sea trials.

7 - 11 November
Queen Mary 2 undertakes Owner's Trials.

22 December
Queen Mary 2 handed over to Cunard.

2004

8 January
Queen Mary 2 is officially named in Southampton.

12 January
Queen Mary 2 departs on her 14-day Maiden Voyage from Southampton to Fort Lauderdale.

16 April
Queen Mary 2 departs on her Maiden Transatlantic Crossing to New York.

The funnel goes on

BRITANNIA RESTAURANT

Saturday 17 April 2004

CANYON RANCH SPACLUB SELECTIONS

Spinach and Pear Salad with Rosemary Vinaigrette

● Stuffed Eggplant with Olive Vinaigrette, Roasted Artichokes,
Cherry Tomatoes & Pine Nuts

Berries with Lemon Curd

~

APPETIZERS & SOUPS

Sevruga Caviar with Classical Garnish

● Chilled Cantaloupe Melon Tartar, Citrus & Mint Marmalade, Basil Jelly

Steamed Black Mussels, Saffron Velouté

Shrimp Bisque With Corn Custard, Baby Shrimp

Chicken Consommé & Matzo Balls

~

SALADS

● Radicchio Salad & Blood Oranges

● Chicory & Flaked Blue Cheese, Apple Sherry Dressing

● Indicates dishes suitable for Vegetarians

17

ENTREES

Fettuccine with Chicken, Goat's Cheese & Spinach

Mediterranean Seabass, Lobster Medallion, Roasted Vegetables, Olive Tapenade

Roast Capon, Chipolata Stuffing & Sage Gravy

Grilled Beef Tenderloin Steak, Creamed Parsnips & Ricotta Cake

● Pressed & Seared Tofu on Red Lentil Curry

~

DESSERTS

Floating Island with Bourbon Vanilla Cream

Nougat Glace with Caramelized Pears and Strawberries

Baked Alaska with Warm Cherry Compote

Sugar Free - Strawberry Mousse with Fresh Berry Salad

Butter Pecan and Vanilla Ice Cream with Chocolate Frozen Yogurt, Mint Sauce

Cheese Selection with Munster, Brie, Stilton, Gloucester

CUNARD

These days it is easy to overlook the enormity of Samuel Cunard's original achievements. Born in Halifax, Nova Scotia, he successfully ran a coastal shipping company, but he was fascinated by the thought of a regular transatlantic service. So too, was the British Admiralty which was then responsible for carrying the Royal Mail overseas.

Samuel Cunard (1787 - 1865)

When the Admiralty invited shipowners to provide a regular time-tabled Atlantic service, with the lure of a substantial contract for carrying the mail, Samuel Cunard appreciated the potential. However, his fellow businessmen in Halifax did not, and having failed to find partners at home Cunard sailed for Britain on the Falmouth packet on 4 January 1839.

He found British businessmen ready to join in the venture and in May 1839 the final contract with the Admiralty was signed. On 4 July 1840 (the day that Queen Mary 2's keel would be laid exactly 162 years later) the impossibly-named 'British and North American Steam Packet Company' (invariably referred to as Cunard Line) saw its first ship, the tiny 1,156-ton **Britannia**, set sail from Liverpool for Halifax with Samuel Cunard and his daughter on board. The ship arrived to a tumultuous welcome in Halifax 11 days later and arrived in Boston (to an even more ecstatic fanfare) three days afterwards.

Within a year three further ships were added to the fleet, thus establishing the very first scheduled steamer service across the Atlantic – a service which was a maritime continuation of the time-tabled service provided by the relatively new railways on land. Cunard had established the service with commendable speed – just two years after the first truly successful crossing of the Atlantic by a steamship.

Underwritten by his Admiralty contract, Cunard prospered despite increasing competition over the years. While his ships did not set out to be the fastest (despite which the company has held the Blue Riband for over six decades), and although Cunard himself eschewed the marble bathrooms and stately ballrooms favoured by other lines, his safety record attracted a large and loyal clientele. Today the company's safety record remains unparalleled in mass transport; despite having carried millions of passengers millions of miles in more than 200 ships over 160 years, the company has never been responsible for the loss of a single life (or mailbag) in peacetime.

The heyday of passenger liners began towards the end of the 19th Century when the pressure of international competition on the lucrative Atlantic service, led to the development of vessels that rivalled Versailles; even Cunard, whose early rather austere attitude had meant comforts being grudgingly conceded after others had led the way, was inspired to compete in the battle of the grand saloon. From then on came the legendary ships, each bigger, more powerful and more luxurious than the last – Cunard ships like Lusitania, Mauretania and Aquitania, Queen Mary and Queen Elizabeth and then Queen Elizabeth 2.

19

A TRIUMPH OF A GREAT TRADITION

Queen Mary leaves New York for the last time, 22 September 1967. On 22 April 2004 a new Queen Mary will enter New York for the first time.

Cunard ships saw war as well as peacetime service and sustained huge losses during both the First and Second World Wars – 22 in the First, including the Lusitania, and 39 in the Second. During the 1939 – 1945 War the Queen Mary and Queen Elizabeth became the greatest troop carriers ever – moving whole divisions, up to 16,000 men at a time across the world. More recently QE2 carried Five Brigade during the Falklands Conflict.

In 1958 more people crossed the Atlantic by air than by sea for the first time ever. Cunard went into decline like many other well-known shipping companies, but was more fortunate than most. In 1971, after an independent existence of 131 years, Cunard was acquired by Trafalgar House.

The company was expanded but through acquisitions rather than newbuilds. After several further changes in ownership, by the mid 1990s, the Cunard fleet was an eclectic mix of vessels with the last one built for the company being QE2 which had entered service in 1969.

In 1998, Cunard was acquired by Carnival Corporation, the largest cruise group in the world. Almost immediately, plans were developed for a new ocean liner which eventually became Queen Mary 2.

Cunard has travelled a long way – literally and figuratively – in the last 164 years and its present position says much about the company's commitment to high standards of all kinds – in customer care and fine seamanship.

CUNARD

Embarkation Recipes

Spinach and Pear Salad with Rosemary Vinaigrette

Ingredients

2 tablespoons red wine vinegar

2 tablespoons rice wine vinegar

2 tablespoons vegetable broth

1 ½ tablespoons minced shallots

2 teaspoons white miso

1 tablespoon chopped fresh parsley

1 ½ teaspoons chopped fresh rosemary

4 cups baby spinach

4 teaspoons coarsely chopped toasted walnuts

2 pears, unpeeled, cored, thinly sliced

¼ cup crumbled blue cheese

Instructions

Blend vinegars, broth, shallots and miso in a blender until smooth.

Mix in the herbs, and season to taste with salt and pepper.

Toss spinach and walnuts in a large bowl and coat with dressing.

Place spinach on salad plates.

Top with sliced pears and cheese.

Stuffed Eggplant with Olive Vinaigrette, Roasted Artichokes, Cherry Tomatoes & Pine Nuts

Stuffed Eggplants

Ingredients (4 servings)

2 small eggplants

1 cup tomato, peeled and diced

4 cloves garlic, chopped

6 ounces zucchini, chopped

½ cup cooked rice

2 tablespoons chopped fresh oregano

1 tablespoon chopped fresh parsley

½ teaspoon freshly ground black pepper

¼ teaspoon salt

2 tablespoons freshly grated Pecorino Romano cheese

2 tablespoons bread crumbs

Olive oil spray

Instructions

Preheat oven to 400°F.

Cut eggplants in half lengthwise.

Leaving a ¼ inch shell all around, scoop out and dice the pulp.

Preheat a medium skillet over medium-high heat.

Add the tomato and garlic.

Stirring constantly, heat mix to bubbling.

Add zucchini and diced eggplant

Cook for 6 minutes, stirring occasionally.

As mixture softens and almost dries, stir in the rice, oregano, black pepper, and salt.

Fill each eggplant half with a mounded ½ cup of the mixture.

Place in a baking dish, cover, and bake for 15 minutes.

Mix cheese, bread crumbs, and parsley together.

Remove the baking dish from the oven.

Spray the stuffed eggplants with a light mist of olive oil.

Sprinkle each eggplant with 4 teaspoons of bread crumb mix.

Return to oven and bake, uncovered, for 15 minutes, or until browned.

Olive Vinaigrette

Ingredients

3 anchovy fillets

1 garlic clove

½ small shallot, minced

2 tablespoons lemon juice

1 tablespoon red wine vinegar

Freshly ground black pepper

½ cup pitted olives, finely chopped

2 tablespoons minced parsley

¼ cup extra virgin olive oil

Instructions

Finely chop the anchovy and garlic.

Mash into a paste with the side of a chef's knife.

Add the minced shallot, lemon juice and vinegar to the paste in a bowl.

Season with pepper, and let stand for 10 minutes.

Add the chopped olives, parsley and olive oil.

Whisk thoroughly.

Drizzle vinaigrette over the cooked eggplant.

This vinaigrette improves with age. It can be made a few days ahead and refrigerated until use.

Roasted Artichokes

Ingredients (4 servings)

8 jumbo artichokes

12 cloves garlic, thinly sliced

1 cup almonds, thinly sliced

3 tablespoons sea salt

3 tablespoons freshly ground black pepper

2 lemons, zested, seeded, peeled, and finely chopped

1 ½ cups fresh oregano leaves

1 ½ cups extra-virgin olive oil

Instructions

Preheat grill.

Trim tops and tips of artichokes by 1 ½ inches.

Mix garlic, almonds, salt, pepper, lemons and oregano thoroughly in a bowl.

Spread artichokes open and stuff the oregano mixture between the leaves.

Drizzle 4-5 tablespoons of olive oil over each artichoke.

Grill for 1 hour, turning every 10-15 minutes.

The outer base will look charred, but the insides will be fully cooked.

Cherry Tomatoes and Pine Nuts

Ingredients (4 servings)

2 tablespoons pine nuts

2 tablespoons olive oil

1 shallot, sliced

1 pint cherry tomatoes, halved

2 tablespoons sherry vinegar

Instructions

In a dry skillet, cook pine nuts over medium heat, stirring often until toasted.

Set aside pine nuts and in the same skillet, heat olive oil over medium-high heat.

Add shallots and cook for 3 minutes stirring constantly, until golden

Add tomatoes and cook for 1 minute.

Stir in vinegar and cook for 1 minute stirring constantly.

Sprinkle with nuts and serve.

Berries with Lemon Curd

Ingredients (6 servings)

4 lemons

6 large egg yolks

1 cup sugar

6 tablespoons cold butter, diced

¼ cup limoncello liqueur, plus extra for sprinkling berries

3 cups assorted berries, washed and dried

3 tablespoons crème fraiche

6 sprigs of fresh mint

Instructions

Finely grate lemon for 2 teaspoons of lemon zest.

Squeeze lemons for ½ cup juice.

Strain through a fine strainer and set aside.

Fill a medium saucepan to a 1 ½ inch depth of water.

Bring to a simmer over medium-high heat.

In a heat-resistant bowl, whisk the egg yolks and sugar until pale and slightly thick.

Add the lemon zest and fresh lemon juice. Whisk thoroughly.

Place the bowl with the egg mixture over the simmering water and whisk constantly until mix thickens. Whisk until the mixture turns light yellow and coats the back of a spoon.

Remove bowl from heat. Whisk the diced butter into the curd. Allow each tablespoon to fully merge before adding the next.

Stir in the limoncello.

Strain the curd through a wire-mesh strainer and place in a clean container.

Cover with plastic wrap. Press wrap onto the surface of the curd to prevent a skin forming.

Chill completely.

Sprinkle berries with limoncello and toss gently. Let stand for a few minutes to macerate.

Put ½ cup berries into each of 6 small serving dishes.

Top each with 1/3 cup of chilled curd.

Garnish each portion with crème fraiche and a sprig of fresh mint.

Sevruga Caviar with Classical Garnish

Ingredients (6 servings)

18 small new potatoes

3 tablespoons melted butter

2 tablespoons chives, minced

2 oz Sevruga caviar

7 oz crème fraiche

Instructions

Wash potatoes well. Place in a large pot of cold salted water.

Bring potatoes to a boil on high heat, and then lower to a

simmer.

Cook potatoes for 10-15 minutes until just tender

Drain and cool in a colander until all moisture steams off.

Cut potatoes in half. Chop off each end of the potatoes

enough to sit still on a plate.

Scoop out potatoes enough to hold the crème and caviar.

Toss the potatoes halves with melted butter.

season to taste with salt and fresh ground pepper.

Arrange potatoes on serving plates and spoon crème fraiche

into the hollows.

Top with caviar and sprinkle with chives.

Serve warm.

Chilled Cantaloupe Melon Tartar, Citrus & Mint Marmalade, Basil Jelly

Ingredients (6 servings)

½ cup mint marmalade (recipe follows)

2 tablespoons fresh lemon juice

1 large honeydew melon, well chilled

Instructions

In small saucepan, combine marmalade and lemon juice.

Heat over medium-low heat until melted.

Cut melon into 6 wedges. Remove and throw away seeds.

Place on chilled dessert plates.

Drizzle the warm sauce over the chilled melon and serve.

Mint Marmalade

Ingredients

2 pounds Granny Smith apples

1 quart water

½ cup lemon juice

2 cups fresh mint leaves

sugar

green food coloring

Instructions

Cut the whole apples into thick slices. Do not peel or core them.

Bring apples, water, lemon juice and mint leaves to a boil in a large saucepan.

Simmer uncovered for 10 minutes.

Mash the apples with a wooden spoon.

Boil for another 15 minutes until they turn to pulp.

Strain the mixture through cheesecloth into a bowl.

Let the bowl sit overnight.

Measure the juice and pour it back into the saucepan.

Add 1 cup of warmed up sugar for each measured cup of juice.

Stir over heat until the sugar dissolves.

Boil until the mixture sets.

Tint with a few drops of food coloring, until it is the desired green.

Remove from heat and let sit for a few minutes.

Pour the mixture into warmed sterile jars.

When cool, seal and label the jars with date made.

Steamed Black Mussels, Saffron Veloute

Ingredients (6 servings)

6 dozens mussels, scrubbed and debearded

1 ½ cups dry white wine

12 parsley sprigs

1 ½ ounces butter

2 tablespoons flour

2 cups fish stock

¼ teaspoon salt

1 pinch white pepper

Instructions

Combine mussels, wine and parsley sprigs in Dutch oven.

Cover and cook over high heat until mussels open up.

Discard any unopened mussels.

Transfer remaining mussels to a bowl and set aside juice.

Melt the butter in a large skillet

Add flour, and cook over low heat.

When the roux is slightly brown, slowly blend in the fish stock.

Whip until smooth.

Bring to a boil, stirring occasionally, until the sauce thickens.

Simmer 10 minutes

Season to taste with salt and pepper.

Add mussels to skillet.

Stir, heat mussels thoroughly and serve.

Shrimp Bisque with Corn Custard, Baby Shrimp

Shrimp Bisque

Ingredients (6 servings)

1 pound whole shrimp, peeled

1 bay leaf

1 small onion, skinned

1 small carrot, peeled

2 tablespoons tomato purée

1 sprig of fresh parsley

1 ¾ pints fish stock

1 ounce butter

1 ounce flour

salt and pepper

4 tablespoons single cream

3 tablespoons brandy

Instructions

Dice the carrot and chop up the onion.

Place in pan with the bay leaf, parsley, tomato purée and fish stock.

Bring to a boil, cover and then simmer for 30 minutes.

Filter mixture through a sieve to smooth it and return pan after rinsing.

Mix the butter with the flour until evenly blended and creamy.

Add to the soup in small dollops one at a time.

Bring to a boil over moderate heat stirring continually.

Lower to a simmer and stir for 2 minutes until thick and smooth.

Hold a few shrimps back for garnish and stir the remainder into the bisque.

Add brandy and cream, then heat and stir gently for one minute.

Season to taste with salt and pepper.

Serve into pre-warmed soup dishes.

Float the garnish shrimps on top of the bisque and serve hot.

Corn Custard

Ingredients (6 servings)

2 ½ cups corn kernels

½ sweet red pepper

4 eggs

¾ cup light sour cream

½ cup shredded aged cheddar cheese

½ teaspoon salt

¼ teaspoon pepper

Instructions

Preheat oven to 350°F.

Chop the pepper, and beat the eggs.

Grease a shallow casserole dish

Sprinkle the corn and red pepper into the casserole dish

Whisk eggs, sour cream, cheese, salt, and pepper together.

Pour mix over corn and peppers.

Bake in oven 1 hour

Remove from oven when top is slightly puffed and golden brown.

Chicken Consommé & Matzo Balls

Chicken Consommé

Ingredients (6 servings)

8 ounces ground chicken breast

4 ounces yellow onion

2 ounces celery

2 ounces carrots

4 egg whites

4 ounces chopped tomato

12 inch cheesecloth and butcher's twine

6 cups chicken stock

1 fresh parsley sprig, chopped

2 fresh thyme sprigs, chopped

1 clove

1 bay leaf

salt and black pepper

Instructions

Make a sachet by laying cheesecloth flat and adding parsley, thyme, clove and bay leaf.

Tie off, then fasten one end of the twine to the handle of a stock pot.

Julien the onion.

Whisk egg whites and mix ground chicken in.

Add onion, celery, carrots, tomato and herb sachet.

Add the cold chicken stock to the stock pot with the meat.

Heat to 140 degrees. Stir occasionally.

A raft of clearmeat will form.

Poke a small vent hole into the raft. Try not to poke particles back into the consommé.

Remove stockpot from the full heat. Leave the pot standing half on and half off the stovetop.

Cook the soup to 140 degrees over low to medium low heat as the liquid filters itself through the clearmeat raft.

Add salt and pepper to taste. Add it one top of the raft to filter in without clouding the consommé.

Julien the carrots and celery, cut into a brunoise of tiny cubes and place in soup dishes.

Strain the consommé through cheesecloth, and heat until piping hot.

Strain liquid through cheesecloth again to ensure consommé is clear, light, and amber color.

Pour the consommé into the soup dishes, add Matzo Balls (recipe follows) and serve.

Matzo Balls

Ingredients

3/8 cup chicken broth

3/8 cup melted butter

½ pound matzo meal

1 ½ teaspoons salt

½ teaspoon ground white pepper

5 eggs

Instructions

Combine chicken broth and butter together.

Mix in matzo meal, salt and pepper.

Add eggs and mix completely.

Cover and refrigerate for 30 minutes.

Boil 2 quarts lightly salted water in a large pot.

Roll matzo mixture into balls of the desired density.

Drop the matzo balls into the boiling water.

Boil for 30 minutes.

Drain and add to consommé.

Radicchio Salad & Blood Oranges

Ingredients (4 servings)

2 heads radicchio

2 teaspoons olive oil

2 teaspoons balsamic vinegar

1 teaspoon Dijon mustard

4 ounces blood oranges

Instructions

Peel and segment oranges.

Trim and wash radicchio leaves.

Whisk oil, vinegar and mustard, in a large bowl, until thoroughly mixed.

Add radicchio, toss until well coated.

Place on salad plates.

Garnish with a topping of orange slices.

Serve immediately.

Chicory & Flaked Blue Cheese, Apple Sherry Dressing

Chicory & Flaked Blue Cheese

Ingredients (4 servings)

2 large heads of chicory

4 ounces flaked blue cheese

1 green pepper, seeded and chopped

2 sticks of celery, cleaned and chopped

4 ounces radishes, trimmed and sliced

4 ounces walnut halves

Instructions

Clean and trim chicory, chop coarsely.

Put the chicory and flaked cheese in a large bowl.

Add pepper, celery and sliced radish, mix thoroughly.

Toss with dressing (recipe follows) until well coated.

Top off with a sprinkling of walnuts.

Apple Sherry Dressing

Ingredients (4 servings)

2 ounces plus 1 tablespoon balsamic vinegar

2 ounces plus 1 tablespoon turbinado sugar

2 teaspoons of honey

3 sprigs thyme, chopped

2 ounces plus 1 tablespoon apple juice

5 ounces grapeseed oil

2 ounces plus 1 tablespoon extra-virgin olive oil

2 tablespoons chopped flat leaf parsley

½ shallot, peeled

1 clove garlic

1 Granny Smith apple

salt and freshly cracked black pepper to taste

Instructions

Finely dice the apple.

In a blender, fully combine all but the apples and herbs.

Add apples and herbs.

Season to taste with salt and pepper

Toss the salad until well coated with vinaigrette.

Serve immediately.

Fettucine with Chicken, Goat's Cheese & Spinach

Ingredients

1 cup dry white wine

2 tablespoons minced shallots

5 ounces crumbled goat cheese, at room temperature

salt and freshly cracked black pepper to taste

1 pinch crushed red chile flakes

8 ounces dried fettuccine

2 skinless, boneless chicken breast halves

2 tablespoons olive oil

4 ounces fresh baby spinach

2 tablespoons chopped fresh basil

Instructions

Place white wine and shallots in a medium saucepan.

Heat on high until the liquid reduces by half.

Whisk the goat cheese into the mixture until smooth.

Season to taste with salt, fresh pepper and chile flakes.

Boil a large pot of salted water over high heat.

Add pasta and boil 10 minutes or until al dente.

Reserve ½ cup of pasta water, drain the remainder and set fettuccini aside.

While the pasta cooks, pound the chicken with a meat mallet.

Flatten breasts to ¾" thickness.

Season to taste with salt and pepper.

Heat 1 tablespoon of olive oil in a sauté pan over medium-high heat.

Add chicken. Sauté 5 minutes each side until browned and cooked through.

Remove chicken from sauté pan.

Add the remaining 1 tablespoon of olive oil and the spinach.

Sauté spinach for 2 minutes until wilted.

Cut the chicken diagonally into strips

In a large bowl, mix the pasta with the goat cheese sauce.

Add the chicken and spinach.

Test and if the pasta is too dry at this point, stir in reserved pasta water until the sauce reaches the desired consistency.

Season to taste with salt and pepper.

Serve in pre-warmed bowls, topped with basil.

Mediterranean Seabass, Lobster Medallion,
Roasted Vegetables, Olive Tapenade

Mediterranean Seabass
Ingredients (4 servings)

2 lemons

3 tablespoons olive oil

1 tablespoon chopped fresh oregano leaves

1 teaspoon ground coriander

1 ¼ teaspoons salt

2 whole sea bass, cleaned and scaled

¼ teaspoon ground black pepper

2 large oregano sprigs

Instructions

Preheat grill over medium heat.

Grate 1 tablespoon of zest and squeeze 2 tablespoons juice from 1 of the lemons.

Cut the other lemon into one half slices and one half wedges.

Stir lemon juice, grated zest, oil, oregano, coriander, and ¼ teaspoon salt in bowl.

Rinse and dry the fish.

Cut 3 slashes in each side of both fish.

Sprinkle inside and out with salt and pepper.

Place lemon slices and oregano sprigs inside the fish and place in baking dish.

Rub half of the oil mixture over the outside of the fish. Set aside remainder.

Let stand at room temperature for 15 minutes.

Lightly grease grill rack and place fish on hot rack.

Cover and cook for 6 to 7 minutes per side, turning once.

When done, fish should be opaque and flake easily when tested with a fork.

Place fish on cutting board

Cut along backbones from head to tail.

Slide a spatula under front top fillets and lift away from backbones, transfer to plates.

Gently pull backbones and ribs from bottom fillets and transfer to plates. Discard bones.

Drizzle remaining oil mixture over cooked fish fillets.

Serve with lemon wedges

Lobster Medallions

Ingredients

1 pound lobster

Salt to taste

1 splash vinegar

Laurel leaves

Freshly ground black pepper

Instructions

Boil a large pot of salted water.

Add lobster, vinegar, laurel and pepper.

Lower the heat and cook for 8 to 10 minutes.

Remove the loin from the cooked lobster.

Cut into medallions.

Garnish fish with lobster medallions.

Roasted Vegetables

Ingredients

2 red bell peppers

1 green bell pepper

2 onions

2 zucchini

8 ounces mushrooms

6 new potatoes, scrubbed

1 teaspoon salt

2 cloves garlic

coarsely ground black pepper

½ teaspoon oregano

½ tablespoon basil

½ teaspoon rosemary

2 tablespoons extra virgin olive oil

Instructions

Preheat oven to 475 degrees.

Mix the peppers, onions, zucchini, mushrooms and potatoes in a large bowl.

Combine the herbs and olive oil in a small bowl.

Drizzle the oil and herbs mixture over the vegetables.

Toss vegetables until well coated.

Season to taste with salt and pepper.

Transfer the vegetable mixture to a large roasting pan

Bake for 35 to 45 minutes, tossing occasionally.

Vegetables will tender and lightly browned when done.

Press garlic cloves.

Squeeze the garlic purée over the oven roasted vegetables.

Serve while hot.

Olive Tapenade

Ingredients

¾ pound pitted black olives

3 to 4 ounces capers, drained and rinsed

2 anchovy fillets, drained, rinsed and patted dry

2 cloves garlic, minced

1 teaspoon Dijon mustard

1 bay leaf, finely chopped

5 sprigs fresh thyme, finely chopped

3 tablespoons chopped parsley

¼ teaspoon crushed red pepper

½ lemon, juiced

1 teaspoon red wine vinegar

1 tablespoon cognac

½ cup extra-virgin olive oil

Instructions

Place all ingredients in the bowl of a food processor.

Process on pulse setting until mixture is coarsely puréed.

Season to taste.

Roast Capon, Chipolata Stuffing & Sage Gravy

Roast Capon

Ingredients

1 capon (8 pounds)

Salt and fresh ground black pepper

¼ pound unsalted butter, softened

2 lemons

2 tablespoons lemon juice

¼ cup fresh chopped thyme

1 onion

4 garlic cloves, smashed

Fresh whole thyme and savory sprigs

2 cups water

Instructions

Preheat oven to 450 degrees.

Remove neck and giblets from the capon, trim excess fat.

Rinse with cold water, inside and out. Pat dry.

Season generously with salt and pepper, including the cavity.

In a small bowl, blend butter, lemon juice and chopped herbs.

Rub the herbed butter all over the capon.

Cut lemons and onion in half.

Place the lemon halves, onion halves, garlic and whole herbs inside the cavity.

Tie legs together with kitchen twine to hold its shape.

Place the capon, breast side down, on a rack in a roasting pan.

Pour water into the pan.

Roast for 20 minutes, then remove from oven.

Turn capon breast side up and baste all over with pan drippings.

Lower heat to 375 degrees.

Return the pan to the oven and roast 2 hours.

When done, a meat thermometer in the thick of the thigh reads 165-170 degrees.

Remove the bird to a serving platter. Let stand for 15 minutes before carving.

Reserve drippings for gravy (recipe follows)

Chipolata Stuffing

Ingredients

12 ounces bulk chipolata sausage meat (recipe follows)

¾ cup finely chopped onion

½ cup chopped green sweet pepper

½ cup chopped celery

½ cup butter

5 cups dry white bread cubes

4 ½ cups crumbled corn bread

1 teaspoon poultry seasoning

1/8 teaspoon black pepper

1 ½ cups chicken broth

Instructions

In a large skillet, brown sausage over medium heat.

Drain, remove from skillet and set aside.

In same skillet, sauté onion, sweet pepper, and celery in hot butter over medium heat until tender.

Set aside.

Combine bread cubes and corn bread in a large bowl.

Add cooked sausage, onion mixture, poultry seasoning and black pepper.

Drizzle with enough broth to moisten.

Toss lightly until combined.

Place mixture into a 2-quart casserole dish.

Cover and bake in a 325 degree oven for 45 minutes or until heated throughout.

Chipolata Sausage

This is the classic English pork sausage, the basic banger.

Ingredients

7 ½ pounds pork butts

1 pound pork fatback

1 tablespoon sage

1 teaspoon dried onion flakes

1 teaspoon thyme

1 teaspoon mace

1 ½ tablespoons salt

6 ounces bread crumbs

1 tablespoon pepper

1 pint water

Instructions

Grind the meat and fatback through a 3/8 plate.

Mix the herbs and seasonings in the water and chill.

Purée the meat in a food processor and chill.

Add the herbs, spices and seasonings to the meat.

Add the bread crumbs and chill the meat mixture.

Set aside 12 ounces of mixture for the chipolata stuffing (recipe above).

Using 28mm casings, stuff the remaining mixture into 1-inch links and refrigerate.

Grill, sauté or cook in the oven, as you prefer and serve at once

Sage Gravy

Ingredients

Reserved drippings (from capon recipe above).

½ cup finely chopped onion

½ cup finely chopped carrot

¼ cup finely chopped celery

1 tablespoon finely chopped fresh sage leaves

1/3 cup Chablis

½ cup chicken broth

1 cup half-and-half (Equal parts milk and cream)

½ teaspoon lemon juice

½ teaspoon salt

½ teaspoon pepper

2 tablespoon cold butter, cut into pieces

Preparation

Mix onion, carrot, celery and chopped sage with drippings in a skillet.

Cook on medium heat, stirring constantly, until onion is tender.

Add wine, bring to a boil, and cook until liquid reduces down to 2 tablespoons.

Add broth, and cook until liquid reduces by half.

Stir in half-and-half.

Return to a boil. Cook until slightly thickened.
Strain mixture through a wire-mesh into a bowl (discard vegetables).

Return mixture to skillet. Stir in lemon juice, salt, and pepper.

Add butter, 1 piece at a time and stir with a wire whisk until fully blended.

Grilled Beef Tenderloin Steak, Creamed Parsnips & Ricotta Cake

Grilled Beef Tenderloin Steak

Ingredients (2 Servings)

1 tablespoon Dijon mustard

1 ½ teaspoons horseradish

¼ teaspoon dried basil

¼ teaspoon dried thyme leaves

¼ teaspoon dried tarragon leaves

¼ teaspoon black pepper

2 (8 ounce) beef tenderloin steaks

Salt to taste

Instructions

Stir mustard, horseradish, basil, thyme, tarragon, and pepper to make a paste.

Spread paste over top and sides of steaks and wrap each steak in plastic wrap.

Marinate steaks in refrigerator overnight.

Preheat oven to 400°F.

Lightly coat a small, glass baking dish with cooking spray.

Unwrap marinated steaks. Season with salt and place in baking dish.

Roast steaks to preference (30 minutes for medium-rare, 1 hour for well done).

Creamed Parsnips

Ingredients

1 pound parsnips

1 dash lemon juice

2 ounces butter

3 ½ fluid ounces water

2 fluid ounces double cream

salt and pepper to taste

Instructions

Peel, core and dice parsnips.

Squeeze lemon juice over diced parsnips.

Melt butter in saucepan to foaming.

Add parsnips to foaming butter.

Stir to coat and then add water.

Cook on low heat for 15 minutes until tender and breaking apart.

Slowly bring the double cream to a very low boil.

Put the parsnips and cream in a blender.

Season to taste with salt and pepper.

Purée until smoothed.

Press through sieve for maximum smoothness.

Serve immediately

Ricotta Cake

Ingredients

butter

1 ¾ cups fresh ricotta

2/3 cup sugar

½ cup candied grated orange zest

½ cup anisette

½ orange, zested

4 tablespoons Fernet Branca amaro

3 eggs, separated

Instructions

Preheat oven to 300 degrees.

Lightly butter a 9-inch cake pan.

Combine ricotta, sugar, candied zest, anisette, orange zest, amaro and egg yolks in a large bowl.

Mix thoroughly with a wooden spoon.

Add egg whites one at a time, mix each in thoroughly.

Pour mixture into buttered cake pan and bake 30 minutes.

When done the top will be a light golden brown.

Serve hot or cold as desired.

Pressed & Seared Tofu on Red Lentil Curry

Ingredients (4 servings)

4 small onions, diced

4 garlic cloves, minced

2 cup red lentils, rinsed and drained

4 tablespoons olive oil

4 cups water

2 pounds pressed or firm tofu

2 teaspoons Cumin seeds

2 teaspoon curry powder

2 teaspoon salt, plus extra to taste

2 tablespoons fresh cilantro, chopped

3 pieces fresh ginger, cut into small thin sticks

Instructions

Heat 2 tablespoons oil in a saucepan.

Cook onions and garlic on medium low heat.

Stir until golden.

Add ginger and cook for one minute.

Add water and lentils. Bring to a boil.

Reduce heat and simmer uncovered for 20 minutes.

Lentils will be soft enough to break apart.

While lentils are cooking, rinse tofu and trim ends.

Cut tofu into small cubes.

Press tofu lightly between paper towels to soak up excess moisture.

Heat remaining 2 tablespoons oil in a wok over medium heat.

Cook cumin seeds 1 minute, stir until aromatic.

Add tofu cubes and leave untouched for 2 minutes.

Stir fry gently until very light browning begins..

Add curry and salt.

Cook for 2 more minutes.

Mix tofu mixture in with the lentils.

Let the curry continue cooking for 5 minutes to fully develop the flavors.

Add salt to taste.

Remove from heat and serve.

Garnish each serving with with cilantro.

Floating Island with Bourbon Vanilla Cream

Floating Island

Ingredients

1 quart milk

1 vanilla bean, split in half lengthways

8 eggs, separated

1 cup sugar

¼ cup dark rum

1 teaspoon vanilla extract

Instructions

Bring the milk and vanilla to a simmer in a large saucepan.

Beat the egg whites in a mixing bowl until peaks form.

Slowly beat in ½ cup sugar.

Continue beating until stiff.

Spoon large servings onto the simmering milk and poach for 3 minutes each side.

Scoop up poached meringues with a slotted spoon. Place on serving plate.

Repeat this process until all the egg whites are poached.

Whisk egg yolks and ½ cup sugar 3 to 4 minutes to ribbon stage.

To test, lift the whisk into the air with some mixture on it.
Mixture will fall back into the bowl in ribbons and slowly
disappear back into the mixture.

Add the warm milk to the egg yolk mixture.

Return the mix to saucepan again.

Cook, over low heat, stirring constantly. Do not let boil.

When done mixture thickens enough to coat a spoon.

Strain.

Add rum and vanilla extract.

Ladle around the poached meringues.

Bourbon Vanilla Cream

Ingredients

1 cup heavy cream

2 tablespoons sugar

½ teaspoon vanilla extract

1 teaspoon bourbon

Instructions

Whip the cream in an electric mixer.

Add sugar, vanilla, and bourbon as it starts to thicken.

Whip 5 minutes until soft peaks form.

Refrigerate until use.

Nougat Glacé with Carmelized Pears and Strawberries

Nougat Glacé

Ingredients

1 ½ cups heavy cream

4 egg whites

¼ cup sugar, plus 1 tablespoon

2 tablespoons water

2 tablespoons honey

¾ cup chopped toasted almonds

¾ cup mixed chopped dried and candied fruit

Instructions

Beat the cream to stiff peaks.

Refrigerate.

Beat the egg whites to stiff peaks.

Sprinkle 1 tablespoon of sugar over top of egg whites.

Beat to a stiff, glossy meringue and set aside.

Add ¼ cup sugar to water and bring to a boil.

Boil for 4 minutes until the syrup forms a ball when put in cold water.

Add honey. Return to boil.

With electric beaters running in the whites, slowly pour syrup into the beaters.

Beat 10 minutes until the meringue is cooled.

Sprinkle fruit and nuts over the meringue.

Add whipped cream on top.

Fold together gently until evenly mixed.

Freeze in a cake pan.

To remove from pan, dip the pan in hot water and flip the nougat onto a serving dish.

Serve with Carmelized Pears and Strawberries (recipe follows).

Carmelized Pears and Strawberries

Ingredients

1 Williams pear

2 tablespoon sugar

2 teaspoon dark Muscovado sugar

2 tablespoons olive oil

4 strawberries, sliced

Instructions

Peel and core pear.

Slice pear thinly and coat in sugar and dark Muscovado sugar.

Caramelize in olive oil on low heat.

Pears are done when they soften.

Toss caramelized pear slices with the strawberries

Serve with nougat. (recipe above)

Baked Alaska with Warm Cherry Compote

Baked Alaska

Ingredients (Serves 6)

1 quart ice cream

3 large eggs

1 cup water

1/3 cup sugar

½ cup flour

2 teaspoons cornstarch

4 egg whites

¾ cup powdered sugar

Instructions

Soften ice cream at room temperature for 1 hour.

Bring water to a simmer over low heat in a small sauce pan.

Preheat oven to 425 degrees.

Beat eggs and sugar in a small steel mixing bowl over simmering water (double boiler), until the temperature reaches 110-120 degrees.

Remove from heat and continue beating until light and creamy and cooled.

Add flour and cornstarch.

Fold gently. Do not over mix.

Place a sheet of wax paper on a greased baking pan.

Spread the sponge base mixture thinly over the wax paper forming a rectangle.

Bake in oven for 5 minutes.

Remove from oven and let cool.

Remove cake from wax paper.

Cover the bottom and sides of your choice of mold with pieces of cake.

Put the softened ice cream on top of the cake to fill the mold.

Cover the top with more cake.

Freeze for 3 hours.

Beat eggwhites and powdered sugar to a stiff meringue.

Place meringue in a piping bag.

Preheat oven to 425 degrees.

Remove frozen ice cream cake from mold and place on baking tray.

Pipe the meringue over top and sides of the cake.

Sculpture meringue as desired.

Bake in the oven for 4 minutes.

Cake is done when meringue edges are browned.

Remove from oven and serve.

The meringue surface should be baked, while the ice cream inside remains frozen.

Warm Cherry Compote

Ingredients

½ cup sugar

4 cups pitted Bing cherries

½ cup water

Instructions

Stir sugar, ½ cup water and cherries together in a large saucepan.

Bring to a low boil.

Cook for 20 minutes.

Compote is done when cherries start to soften.

Remove from heat and let cool.

Serve.

Sugar Free Strawberry Mousse with Fresh Berry Salad

Sugar Free Strawberry Mousse

Ingredients (5 Servings)

8 ounces fresh strawberries

¾ cup Splenda®

1 tablespoon lemon juice

1 tablespoon water

½ teaspoon lemon zest

1 Pinch sea salt

¼ teaspoon vanilla

2 teaspoons unflavored powdered gelatin

1 cup heavy cream

Instructions

Rinse, hull and slice strawberries.

Sprinkle gelatin over a tablespoon of water in a small bowl.

Set aside and let soften.

Purée the strawberries, zest, juice and salt.

Heat purée in a saucepan over medium heat.

Stir Splenda® into strawberries. Heat until hot.

Add gelatin, stir until melted in.

Remove from heat and let cool.

Beat cream to soft peaks.

Beat vanilla into cream.

Gently fold strawberry mixture into cream.

Pour into serving cups

Chill 2 hours before serving.

Fresh Berry Salad

Ingredients

2 cups mixed fresh berries (raspberries, blackberries, blueberries, huckleberries, strawberries, etc. according to season)

6 teaspoons Splenda®

2 drops vanilla extract

1/8 teaspoon cinnamon

1 small pinch salt

Instructions

Rinse and drain berries.

Cut strawberries into quarters.

Place all ingredients in a bowl.

Mix gently with spatula until all berries are coated with Splenda®

Chill covered 1 hour.

While chilling, mix occasionally with any syrup that pools at the bottom of the bowl.

Serve berries with Strawberry Mousse (recipe above).

Pour any remaining syrup over berries.

Butter Pecan and Vanilla Ice Cream with Chocolate Frozen Yogurt, Mint Sauce

Ingredients

1 quart butter pecan ice cream

1 quart vanilla ice cream

1 quart chocolate frozen yogurt

¾ cup light cream

8 ounces semisweet or bittersweet chocolate, chopped

2 tablespoons unsalted butter, cut into small pieces

2 tablespoons white crème de menthe

Instructions

Melt chocolate in the top of double boiler.

Blend in liquor and cream.

Heat chocolate until completely melted.

Remove from heat.

Whisk butter into the melted chocolate sauce..

Scoop ice cream and yoghurt into bowls.

Drizzle chocolate sauce over ice cream.

Serve immediately.

Cheese Selection with Munster, Brie, Stilton, Gloucester

Ingredients

1 wedge Munster cheese

1 wedge Brie cheese

1 wedge Stilton cheese

1 wedge Gloucester cheese

1 package water crackers

1 package butter crackers

1 package sesame crackers

1 package rice crackers

1 package cream crackers

2 small clusters seedless grapes

Instructions

At least half an hour before serving, arrange cheese wedges on cutting board

Provide a separate cheese knife for each cheese.

Place crackers on serving plates next to the cheese board.

Garnish with grapes.

Self-serve.

CHAPTER TWO

Death by Chocolate - Mystery Dinner Theater

You awaken to day 2 of your virtual fantasy cruise on

board the Brilliance of the Seas, in port at the fabulous Greek

island of Santorini. Santorini's spectacular caldera is a

vestige of what was probably the biggest volcanic eruption in

recorded history, believed by some to have caused the

disappearance of Atlantis. The island's violent volcanic history is visible everywhere you look in black-sand beaches, earthquake-damaged dwellings and raw cliffs of lava plunging into the sea. Crystal-clear waters and whitewashed villages perched atop the soaring volcanic cliffs make the island of Santorini a wonder to behold. Many visitors come to Santorini to uncover the mysteries of the lost kingdom of Atlantis, while others revel in its relaxed mountaintop atmosphere to enjoy the scenic waters of the Mediterranean. Today you visit the architectural site of Akrotiri, a once-powerful Minoan kingdom. You see the amazing ruins that have been excavated there, buried some thirty feet below the earth's surface after the eruption of the island's volcano. You discover the ancient city's squares and cobblestone streets and peer into some of the houses and shops. You follow that with a leisurely stroll through the scenic village of Oia, a haven for artists and artisans, explore their shops, and enjoy a drink and a traditional lunch. As the sun sinks into the caldera you return to the ship anticipating the wonderful evening of entertainment Royal Caribbean has in store.

Tonight the ship becomes a murder mystery dinner theatre. Act I is set in the Colony Club on deck 6 as drinks are served. Act II takes place in Portofino's Lounge amidst a fine Italian feast. We won't tell you whodunit but you can puzzle over the crime as you prepare Saltimbocca Alla Romano in your own kitchen.

PORTOFINO

Welcome

to

Death by Chocolate

Murder Mystery
Dinner Theatre

ACT I

Colony Club, Deck 6
Champagne will be served

ACT II

Dinner in the Portofino Restaurant
Red and White wine will be served

Murder Mystery Play written by Diana Rubino

Antipasti Assortiti
A colorful plate of traditional Italian appetizers

Porcini Mushroom Broth
Mushroom Consomme

Cesare
Romaine lettuce with shaved parmesan and herb croutons,
tossed with Cesare dressing

Penne Con Salsa Di Pomodoro
Penne in sun-dried tomato and basil sauce
finished with shaved Pecorino Romano

Saltimbocca Alla Romana
A Roman classic – tender veal medallions topped with thinly
sliced prosciutto and fresh sage, served with
asparagus and wild
mushroom risotto, complemented with Marsala jus

Or

Aragosta Al Forno In Salsa Di Erbe Aromatiche

Succulent baked lobster tail served with frothy herb butter,
steamed potatoes and seasonal vegetables

Tiramisu
Espresso Kahlua cake filled with mascarpone cream,
dusted with cocoa powder

Coffee or Tea

Death by Chocolate Recipes

Antipasti Assortiti

Ingredients

1 pound assorted sliced deli meats (salami, spicy capocollo, prosciutto, mortadella, and bresaola)

½ pound Parmigiano-Reggiano, cut into irregular pieces

Pinzimonio (recipe follows)

Marinated Olives (recipe follows)

Roasted Pepper Salad, (recipe follows)

1 loaf focaccia bread, sliced

Instructions

Arrange the meats, cheeses, and foccacia on a large platter.

Arrange a platter of Pinzimonio.

Place the Marinated Olives and Roasted Red Pepper Salad in small serving bowls.

Serve, allowing guests to choose their own preferred antipasti selections.

Pinzimonio

Ingredients

½ cup olive oil

2 teaspoons salt

1 teaspoon fresh ground black pepper

Assorted vegetables (carrots, celery, fennel bulb, radishes, red and orange bell peppers, and cherry tomatoes according to season)

Instructions

Cut the vegetables into bite size pieces.

Mix the oil, salt, and pepper in a small bowl until well blended.

Arrange the vegetables on a platter.

Serve with the dip.

Marinated Olives

Ingredients

3 tablespoons olive oil

1 tablespoon lemon zest

½ teaspoon dried crushed red pepper flakes

1½ cups Sicilian cracked green olives

1½ cups kalamata olives

2 tablespoon chopped fresh basil leaves

Instructions

Stir the oil, lemon zest, and pepper flakes in a small skillet.

Heat for 1 minute on medium, until aromatic.

Remove from heat.

Add the olives and toss to coat.

Add the basil and toss to coat.

Serve.

Roasted Red Pepper Salad

Ingredients

2 large yellow bell peppers

2 large red bell peppers

2 large green bell peppers

1 small red onion, thinly sliced

6 tablespoons olive oil

3 tablespoons balsamic vinegar

1 tablespoon fresh minced oregano

1 tablespoon fresh minced rosemary

1 tablespoon fresh minced fresh basil

1 tablespoon fresh minced parsley

1 garlic clove, minced

½ teaspoon garlic powder

½ teaspoon cayenne pepper

½ teaspoon pepper

¼ teaspoon salt

1 cup cherry tomatoes, halved

8 ounces fresh mozzarella cheese pearls

5 fresh basil leaves

Instructions

Broil peppers 5 minutes until skins blister.

Rotate peppers a quarter turn.

Repeat all sides are broiled.

Place peppers in a large bowl.

Cover and let stand 20 minutes.

Peel off and discard charred pepper skins.

Cut stems and remove seeds.

Slice peppers into thin strips.

Place peppers in large bowl and add onion.

Whisk the oil, vinegar, herbs, garlic, garlic powder, cayenne, pepper and salt in a small bowl.

Pour mixture over peppers and onions. Toss until fully coated.

Cover and refrigerate 4 hours.

Remove from refrigerator and let peppers reach room temperature.

Serve topped with tomatoes, cheese and basil.

Porcini Mushroom Broth

Ingredients (6 servings)

3 cups water

3 cups dried porcini mushrooms

2 tablespoons olive oil

¾ cup shallots, minced

4½ cups low-salt chicken broth

½ cup dry white wine

3 tablespoons dry Sherry

1½ teaspoons coarse salt

½ teaspoon ground black pepper

¾ cup thinly sliced green onion tops

Instructions

Boil 3 cups water in medium saucepan.

Add porcini and remove from heat.

Soak mushrooms 20 minutes until soft.

Line a strainer with cheesecloth.

Strain liquid into medium bowl.

Mushrooms can be reserved for other use.

Heat oil in large saucepan on medium heat.

Add shallots and reduce heat to medium-low.

Sauté shallots 5 minutes until soft.

Add strained mushroom liquid, chicken broth, wine, Sherry, salt, and pepper.

Bring to a boil.

Reduce heat, cover, and simmer 5 minutes.

Serve immediately.

Cesare Ensalata

Ingredients (6 servings)

6 cloves garlic, peeled

¾ cup mayonnaise

5 anchovy fillets, minced

6 tablespoons shaved Parmesan cheese

1 teaspoon Worcestershire sauce

2 teaspoons Dijon mustard

1 tablespoon lemon juice

Salt and ground black pepper to taste

¼ cup olive oil

4 cups day-old French bread cut into ½ inch cubes

2 tablespoons dried Italian herbs

1 head romaine lettuce, torn into bite-size pieces

Instructions

Mince 3 of the garlic cloves.

Mix garlic with mayonnaise, anchovies and 2 tablespoons of Parmesan cheese in a small bowl.

Mix in the Worcestershire sauce, mustard, and lemon juice.

Season to taste with salt and pepper.

Refrigerate dressing until needed.

Heat oil in large skillet on medium heat.

Cut the remaining 3 garlic cloves into quarters.

Stir cloves in hot skillet until brown.

Remove and set aside garlic and add bread cubes to the hot oil.

Cook, turning often, until lightly browned.

Remove croutons from oil, and season with dried Italian herbs.

Place lettuce in a large bowl and toss with dressing, remaining Parmesan cheese, and the herbed croutons.

Serve immediately.

Penne Con Salsa Di Pomodoro

Ingredients

3 tablespoons butter

2 tablespoons olive oil

10 sun-dried tomatoes, cured in oil, chopped

¼ cup fresh basil

¼ cup fresh parsley

4 garlic cloves, minced

Salt and pepper to taste

¼ cup shaved Pecorino Romano

1 pound penne pasta

Instructions

Boil a large pot of water on high heat.

Cook pasta in boiling water until al dente, and then drain.

While pasta is cooking, heat butter and oil in a skillet on medium heat.

Add tomatoes, basil, parsley, and garlic.

Sauté for 10 minutes.

Add salt and pepper to taste.

Serve over warm pasta and finish with a sprinkling of shaved Pecorino Romano cheese.

Saltimbocca Alla Romano

Saltimbocca Alla Romano

Ingredients (4 servings)

4 thin sliced 5-ounce cutlets of veal

4 slices thin sliced prosciutto

8 fresh sage leaves, plus extra sage for garnish

All-purpose flour

Salt and freshly ground black pepper

2 tablespoons extra-virgin olive oil

2 tablespoons unsalted butter

2 tablespoons dry white wine

¼ cup chicken broth

Lemon wedges, for garnish

Instructions

Place veal cutlets side by side on a sheet of plastic wrap.

Place one slice of prosciutto on top of each cutlet

Cover with a second sheet of plastic wrap.

Gently flatten the cutlets with a rolling pin.

Roll until cutlets are ¼ inch thick and the prosciutto sticks to the veal.

Remove the plastic wrap.

Place 2 sage leaves atop the center of each cutlet.

Thread a toothpick through the veal to keep the prosciutto and sage in place.

Put flour in a shallow platter.

Season to taste with salt and pepper.

Mix with a fork to combine and then dredge the veal in the seasoned flour.

Shake off any excess flour.

Heat the oil with 1 tablespoon of butter in a large skillet on medium heat.

Place the cutlets in the skillet, prosciutto-side down.

Cook for 3 minutes until prosciutto is crisp.

Turn over and sauté for 2 minutes, until golden.

Remove cutlets to serving plates.

Take out toothpicks and keep plates warmed.

Add the wine to the skillet.

Stir to bring out the veal flavors from the pan.

Heat to reduction for 1 minute.

Add chicken broth and remaining tablespoon of butter.

Swirl the skillet until butter blends in.

Season to taste with salt and pepper.

Pour sauce over the saltimbocca.

Garnish with remaining sage leaves and lemon wedges

Serve immediately.

Asparagus and Wild Mushroom Risotto

Ingredients (8 servings)

½ cup olive oil

2 tablespoons unsalted butter

4 garlic cloves, minced

½ bunch asparagus

2 cups wild mushrooms (Porcini, Shitake, etc.)

2 cups uncooked Arborio rice

1 cup Riesling wine

4 cups mushroom broth

2 cups water

sea salt and pepper

1 cup Pecorino Romano cheese

Instructions

Break off any hard ends and cut asparagus diagonally into 1 inch pieces

Heat broth and water together in a small pan until simmering

In a large pot, melt butter and olive oil together.

Add mushrooms and sauté 5 minutes.

Add asparagus pieces, garlic and rice.

Stir to coat in oil and butter mix.

Sauté 5 minutes, stir often.

Add Riesling and cook 2 minutes.

Add salt and pepper to taste.

Scoop 2 ladlefuls of broth and water into the mixture and stir on low heat.

Simmer to cook rice, monitoring frequently.

If mixture becomes dry, add 2 more ladlefuls of broth and water.

Continue this procedure until rice is cooked.

After 30 minutes rice will be moist and creamy.

Remove the pot from the heat and add the Pecorino Romano.

Drizzle with olive oil, garnish with parsley, and sprinkle extra cheese on top.

Serve while hot.

Marsala Jus

Ingredients (6 servings)

2 tablespoons butter

2 cups chicken stock

1 sprig fresh thyme

Salt and fresh cracked black pepper

1 clove garlic

¾ cup Marsala wine

2 shallots

Instructions

Chop garlic and slice shallots.

Place in a small saucepan with the thyme.

Sauté in just enough butter to cook.

Deglaze with Marsala and reduce to a syrup.

Add chicken stock and simmer.

Simmer until reduced by one half.

Add salt and pepper to taste.

Strain and return to saucepan.

Whisk in the rest of the butter.

Serve

Aragosta Al Forno in Salsa Di Erbe Aromatica

Baked Lobster Tails

Ingredients (2 Servings)

2 lobster tails

4 tablespoons butter, cut into small pieces

1 clove garlic, minced

2 sprigs rosemary

Salt and pepper

Instructions

Preheat oven to 350°F.

Place a lobster tail on a cutting board belly side down.

With a sharp knife, cut through the back of the lobster tail almost to the end.

Separate the lobster meat from the shell. Keep the tail flesh as intact as possible.

The meat should remain attached to the end of the tail.

Arrange nicely on top of the shell.

Repeat for second lobster tail.

Place the lobster tails in a baking dish.

Spread butter pieces around the lobster tails

Sprinkle garlic around the dish.

Add the rosemary right next to the lobster tails.

Season to taste with salt and pepper.

Bake dish in the oven for 8 minutes.

When done, butter melts and the lobster meat is white.

Remove dish from oven and place the lobster tails serving plates.

Pour Frothy Herbed butter over each tail. (recipe follows).

Frothy Herbed Butter

Ingredients

4 tablespoons butter

2 tablespoons fresh basil, finely chopped

Instructions

Melt butter in a medium saucepan.

Whisk the butter nonstop as it melts.

Remove the butter from the heat before it turns brown.

Continue to whisk.

Add basil.

Whisk briskly until froth forms.

Spoon the butter foam onto the baked lobster (recipe above).

Do not prepare ahead, as froth will fall before you can serve it.

Steamed Potatoes & Seasonal Vegetables

Ingredients

5 large carrots, peeled

4 medium potatoes, quartered

12 Brussels sprouts, halved

1 tablespoon butter, melted

1 tablespoon lemon juice

¼ teaspoon fresh ground black pepper

Instructions

Place carrots and potatoes in a steamer

Cover and steam 6 minutes.

Add sprouts and steam 6 minutes more.

Combine butter, lemon juice and pepper

Toss butter mix with steamed vegetables.

Serve

Tiramisu

Ingredients

3 large eggs, separated

¾ cup sugar

8 ounces mascarpone cheese

½ cup heavy cream

2 cups espresso at room temperature

2 tablespoons sweet Marsala wine

6 ounces savoiardi (crisp Italian ladyfingers)

2 tablespoons cocoa powder

Instructions

Beat egg yolks and ½ cup sugar in a large bowl until thickened and pale.

Beat in mascarpone until barely combined.

Beat whites with a pinch of salt in a separate bowl until they barely hold soft peaks.

Gradually add remaining ¼ cup sugar continuing to beat whites until they barely hold stiff peaks. Beat heavy cream in a separate bowl until it barely holds soft peaks.

Gently fold cream into mascarpone mixture until thoroughly mixed.

Fold in egg whites.

Stir espresso and Marsala wine together in a shallow bowl.

Dip 1 savoiardi into espresso mix and for a few seconds each side.

Place dipped savoiardi in a 2-quart glass baking dish.

Dip 8 more savoiardi and arrange in a snug layer in bottom of dish.

Spread half the mascarpone mixture evenly over dipped savoiardi.

Repeat process to make a second layer of dipped savoiardi and mascarpone.

Cover and chill 6 hours.

Sprinkle with cocoa powder and serve.

Cocktails

Of course Italy is world-famous for its magnificent works of art. Italians are just as

proud of their cocktails, also a form of artistry. In the 1950s, cocktails became fashion

statements along with poodle skirts, cat-eye sunglasses and pompadours. Italy's cocktails-and the glasses they're served in-are as groundbreaking as the fashions on the runways of Milan. Sip a Rossini or a Bellini in a cafe under a star-strewn Roman sky, just as the decadent

Roman emperors did thousands of years ago. Here are four of the most iconic Italian cocktails:

Cardinale

A delicious pre-dinner aperitif.

Ingredients

Gin

Dry Vermouth

Campari

Instructions

Mix 5 parts Gin, 3parts Dry Vermouth and 2 parts Campari.

Pour into a chilled glass filled with ice.

Stir and serve

Bellini

Enjoyable any time of day.

Ingredients

Nettare di pesca (peach juice)

Spumante Brut

Instructions

Build the cocktail in a Champagne flute.

Pour 3 parts peach juice.

Add 7 parts Spumante Brut.

Rossini

Another all-day delight. This is a variation of the Bellini.

Other variations include _Mimosa_ (orange juice and Spumante Brut), _il Tiziano_ (grape juice and Spumante Brut) and _il Puccini_ (mandarin juice and Spumante Brut).

Ingredients

Nettare di fragole (strawberry juice)

Spumante Brut

Instructions

Build the cocktail in a Champagne flute.

Pour 3 parts strawberry juice.

Add 7 parts Spumante Brut.

God Father

Savor as an after dinner treat. For a _God Mother_ substitute vodka for whisky.

Ingredients

Amaretto di Saronno

Scotch whisky

Instructions

Mix 3 parts Amaretto and 7 parts whisky.

Pour into a chilled glass filled with ice.

Stir and serve

CHAPTER THREE

Captain's Gala Dinner

It's day 3 of your virtual fantasy cruise and your eyes
open to your luxury cabin on the 2,000-passenger Armonia,
added to the exclusive Italian cruise line MSC's fleet in
2001. Each ship has a musical name, such as Musica,
Sinfonia, Lyrica, Melody, Rhapsody, and Opera. The
Armonia is moored at the port of Funchal, capital of
Portugal's green and enchanting Madeira Islands. This
morning you opt for a shore excursion. You visit Pico da

Torre to enjoy the view over Camara de Lobos, a typical fishing village. Next you marvel at the amazing Cabo Girao. At 580 meters it is the second highest sea cliff in the world. On to Encumeada summit, 1007 meters high, where both sides of the island (north and south) can be seen at the same time. After lunch you move on to Porto Moniz to discover one of the most beautiful points of the north coast, a road built on the rocks by the sea where you admire the astonishing waterfalls. The village itself is well known for its volcanic swimming pools. A final stop at Paul da Serra, the island's only plateau, 1400 meters above sea level, and then back to Funchal.

After taking a turn at the simulation golf range, and savoring a pint of English ale in the White Lion British Pub on the Rubino Deck it's time for The Captain's Gala Dinner. Suitably attired you enter La Pergola restaurant, featuring fine Italian wines such as white Torre di Giano of Umbria and red Dolcetto d'Alba Scrimaglio from Piemonte.

The understated black and white menu belies the tasty

treats awaiting you. The Chef's Recommendation today is Roses of Norwegian salmon, Crepes filled with ricotta cheese and spinach in pink sauce, and the Antipasti include grilled asparagus on puff pastry toast with Tarragon sauce.

The zuppe (soups) include parmantier cream soup served with buttered croutons, and of course no Italian menu is complete without a pasta dish—Pasta e il Riso—pasta and rice, or Risotto with green apple and champagne.

MSC Armonia
Captain's Gala Dinner

Our Chef's Recommendation
Roses of Norwegian salmon
Crepes filled with ricotta cottage cheese and spinach, in pink sauce
Beef medallion
Baked Alaska

Healthy Choices
Roses of Norwegian salmon
Parmantier cream soup, croutons with butter
Broiled marinated lobster and rice creole
Fresh fruit

Vegetarian Suggestion
Grilled asparagus on puff pastry toast
Risotto with green apple and Champagne
Pojarsky vegetables
Fresh fruit

Menu

Antipasti - Appetizers

Thin slices of Parma raw ham with an exotic fruit fun

Roses of Norwegian salmon, served with rustic salad and croutons with caper pâté

Grilled asparagus on puff pastry toast, Tarragon sauce

Zuppe - Soups

Consommé Denise with Tortellini

Parmantier cream soup served with buttered croutons

Pasta e il Riso - Pasta and Rice

Crepes filled with ricotta cottage cheese and spinach, in pink sauce

Risotto with green apple and champagne

Secondi Piatti - Main Course

Broiled marinated lobster and rice creole

Beef medallion served on bread croutons and mushroom sauce

Baked lamb loin aromatized with herbs and mint sauce

Pojarsky vegetables served with cheese fondue

Vegetali - Vegetables
Potatoes croquettes - Vegetables of the day

Insalata - Salads
Spanish salad
Mushrooms, cherry tomatoes, green beans, onion rings and
salami chorizo

Formaggi - Cheeses
Offered with salted, unsalted and whole-grain cracker, walnuts
and dried fruit

Dolci e Gelato - Desserts & Gelati
Baked Alaska alla flamma
Small assorted pastries
Tropical ice cream cup
Vanilla ice cream with rhum, coconut, raisins and whipped
cream

Frutta - Fruit
Fresh fruit

IL PANE ITALIANO - THE BREADS OF

ITALY
Home - made bread - Sesame bread - Grissini

Tea and American coffee available as required - please ask your waiter

Captain's Gala Recipes

Thin Slices of Parma Raw Ham with an Exotic Fruit Fun

Ingredients (4 servings)

8 slices Parma raw ham (recipe follows)

4 tablespoons ricotta cheese

4 tablespoons wild honey

16 fresh figs

1 tablespoon brown sugar

mixed tropical fruits for garnishment (melon, papaya, pineapple, kiwis, etc.)

Instructions

Score the figs on top and gently squeeze to open them up into florets.

Wrap prosciutto around the open figs.

Spoon ricotta into the openings.

Sprinkle sugar on the ricotta, and place under hot grill.

Remove from heat when figs are warm and cheese begins to turn brown.

Drizzle honey over figs.

Arrange with fresh tropical fruit slices.

Serve immediately.

Parma Raw Ham (prosciutto crudo)

Ingredients (1 whole Parma raw ham)

1 pork leg with bone

12 ounces coarse sea salt

warm water

1½ ounces coarse ground black pepper

10 ounces lard

1 length rope.

1 horse-bone needle

1 meat hook

Instructions

Trim away the fat and muscle from the ham until it is a traditional ham shape.

Apply dry salt to exposed flesh and moistened salt to remaining skin.

Screw meat hook into the ceiling of a refrigerated chamber or walk-in refrigerator.

Tie rope around middle of meat and hang the ham from the meat hook.

Refrigerate at 39 degrees F for 1 week.

Brush away excess salt.

Reapply salt and rehang the ham for 18 days.

Lower temperature to 34 degrees F.

Hang for 70 more days to "rest" the ham.

Wash the ham thoroughly with warm water.

Air dry.

Cure the ham for 3 months in an open, well aired room on a wooden rack.

Mix lard with a little salt and pepper.

Coat the ham with the lard to prevent it drying too quickly.

Cure on the rack for another 6 months.

Insert horse-bone needle, and check the smell and appearance of the ham.

If it has a spicy, sweet aroma it is done.

Finish curing in cellar for 2 years.

Ham is ready to eat.

Roses of Norwegian Salmon, with Rustic Salad and Croutons with Caper Pâté

Roses of Norwegian Salmon

Ingredients (8 servings)

16 ounces smoked Norwegian salmon slices

Instructions

Lay smoked salmon flat.

With a fillet knife, cut a 3-inch-long strip 1 inch wide.

Cut the strip from the edge of the fish, so the naturally uneven edge is part of the strip.

Roll the first inch of the strip tightly to form the center of a rose.

Roll the rest of the strip more loosely around the center.

Pinch together at the cut edge, leaving the thin, uneven edge to form the petals.

Hold the rose at the base.

With the tip of the fillet knife, gently peel back the rolled salmon just enough to open up the rose.

Repeat as necessary until all the salmon is used.

Rustic Salad

Ingredients (8 servings)

½ cup plus 2 tablespoons extra virgin olive oil

3 tablespoons fresh lemon juice

4 ounces prosciutto, chopped

1 ½ cups seedless red grapes

½ cup dried cherries

10 cups mixed greens - frisée, arugula, and torn radicchio

2 Bosc pears

aged balsamic vinegar

½ cup pine nuts, toasted

4 ounces Pecorino Romano cheese

Instructions

Preheat oven to 350°F.

Whisk ½ cup olive oil and lemon juice in small bowl.

Season to taste with salt and pepper.

Set aside for dressing.

Heat 1 tablespoon olive oil in large skillet on medium heat.

Sauté prosciutto until crisp.

Remove and drain crisped prosciutto on paper towels.

Toss grapes with 1 tablespoon olive oil on a baking sheet.

Roast grapes in oven for 15 minutes.

Grapes are done when they just begin to shrivel.

Remove and let grapes cool on baking sheet.

Place cherries in small bowl.

Add hot water until cherries are covered by 1 inch.

Let cherries soak 15 minutes to soften.

Drain cherries and set aside.

Core both pears.

Cut one pear into matchsticks.

Thinly slice remaining pear.

Cut Pecorino Romano into 1/8-inch-thick rectangular slices.

Cut each cheese slice diagonally into triangles

Mix greens, pear matchsticks, dressing, 2/3 of prosciutto, grapes, and cherries in large bowl. Season to taste with salt and pepper.

Place on serving plates.

Garnish with pear slices.

Drizzle with aged balsamic vinegar.

Top with sprinkled pine nuts and remaining prosciutto.

Garnish with cheese.

Serve

Croutons

Ingredients

3 tablespoons olive oil

1 large day-old baguette

1 teaspoon salt

Instructions

Cut bread into 1-inch cubes.

Heat 3 tablespoons olive oil in sauté pan on medium heat.

Sauté bread cubes 5 minutes, stirring constantly.

Croutons are done when toasted and golden all around..

Remove and drain croutons on paper towels.

Top rustic salads.

Caper Pâté

Ingredients (8 servings)

1 pound sheep liver

2 ounces butter

6 rashers bacon

1 medium onion, grated

1 clove garlic, crushed

4 fluid ounces port

½ teaspoon salt

1 teaspoon fresh ground black pepper

1/3 cup single cream

1 teaspoon lemon juice

3 tablespoons mayonnaise

1 tablespoon capers

1/8 cup clarified butter

2 tablespoons fresh parsley

Instructions

Remove membrane and slice liver.

Chop parsley.

Finely chop capers

Coarsely chop bacon.

Heat butter in a saucepan on medium heat.

Fry liver in heated butter in a saucepan.

Liver is done when cooked through with no pink remaining.

Add bacon. Fry until crisp.

Add onion and garlic.

Sauté until onion is translucent.

Add port, salt, pepper and cream.

Simmer 3 minutes.

Add lemon juice and mayonnaise.

Transfer to food processor and liquidize.

Add capers and stir until well mixed.

Transfer to ramekin dishes.

Seal tops with clarified butter mixed with parsley.

Grilled Asparagus on Puff Pastry Toast with Tarragon Sauce

Grilled Asparagus

Ingredients (8 servings)

1 pound fresh asparagus spears

1 tablespoon olive oil

salt

fresh ground black pepper

Instructions

Trim asparagus spears.

Preheat grill on high heat.

Lightly coat asparagus with olive oil.

Season to taste with salt and pepper.

Grill on high 3 minutes.

Asparagus is done when it reaches the desired tenderness.

Puff Pastry Toast

Ingredients (8 servings)

3 cups unbleached all-purpose flour

1 cup plain bleached cake flour

6½ sticks unsalted butter, chilled

1½ teaspoons salt

1 cup ice water

Instructions

Dice butter sticks into ½ -inch cubes.

Put flour in mixing bowl.

Add butter and salt.

Blend flour and butter together until butter broken into small lumps.

Blend in water and mix until dough clumps roughly together but butter pieces remain the same.

On a lightly floured work surface, quickly push, pat and roll dough to form a 12-inch by 18-inch rectangle.

Lightly flour top of dough.

Using a pastry sheet, flip the bottom of the rectangle up over the middle.

Flip the top of the rectangle down to cover it.

Lift the dough away from the work surface using a pastry sheet.

Clean the work surface and lightly.

Return the dough to the work surface. Set it with the top flap to your right.

Lightly flour top of the dough, and push, pat and roll again into a rectangle.

Repeat folding as above. (Each "roll-and-fold" operation is called a "turn".

Repeat process 2 more times. (4 "turns" in total).

After the last "turn" you will see flakes of butter scattered below the surface on the dough.

Wrap dough in plastic wrap and place in a plastic bag.

Refrigerate 40 minutes.

Repeat "turn" process 2 more times.

Let dough rest 30 minutes.

Dough is ready for baking when rubbery and difficult to roll.

Pre-heat oven to 400°F.

Unfold pastry on a lightly floured work surface.

Cut pastry sheet into 5-inch squares.

Place pastry squares on a baking sheet.

Prick the pastry squares with a fork.

Bake for 20 minutes or until the toasted pastry squares are toasted golden brown.

Tarragon Sauce

Ingredients (8 servings)

1 tablespoon olive oil

1 cup plain yogurt

½ cup chopped green onions

1 tablespoon fresh tarragon, minced

1 tablespoon mayonnaise

2 teaspoons lime juice

¾ teaspoon hot pepper sauce

Instructions

Combine ingredients in a small bowl.

Stir until well mixed.

Serve over puff pastry toasts, topped with asparagus.

Consommé Denise with Tortellini
Ingredients (8 servings)

15 egg whites

1 pound lean ground chicken

1 onion

½ pound of carrots

½ pound leeks

½ pound celery

1 cup tomato purée

5 black peppercorns

2 bay leaves

½ bunch parsley sprigs

3 fresh thyme sprigs

1 gallon chicken stock

9 ounces cheese tortellini

salt

pepper

Instructions

Dice onion, carrots, leeks and celery into small cubes.

Whip egg whites lightly in a mixing bowl.

Combine ground chicken, diced vegetables, tomato purée, herbs, and spices together.

Mix in egg whites.

Blend chicken stock and meat mix in a stock pot with spigot,

Place stock pot on medium heat.

Heat to 160 degrees F, stirring occasionally, until a raft forms.

Simmer for 90 minutes. Do not allow raft to break up or sink.

Open spigot, pour off and discard enough liquid to remove any sediment.

Line a china cap strainer with 5 layers of cheesecloth.

Strain the liquid slowly through the china cap.

Re-line and re-strain as necessary until liquid becomes a clear consommé.

Add Tortellini to consommé in a large saucepan.

Bring to a boil.

Cook 5 minutes uncovered.

Tortellini is done when tender,

Season to taste with salt and pepper.

Garnish with herb sprigs.

Serve hot.

Parmantier Cream Soup with Buttered Croutons

Parmantier Cream Soup

Ingredients (6 servings)

6 tablespoons heavy cream

8 cups chicken stock

3 cups leeks

4 cups cubed potatoes

4 tablespoons butter

2 onions

1 tablespoon salt

¼ teaspoon pepper

Fresh chives for garnish

Instructions

Clean and dice the white and tender green parts of leeks and onions.

Heat butter in a heavy saucepan.

Sauté leeks and onions until soft and yellow.

Add potatoes, salt, and pepper to chicken stock.

Simmer 50 minutes until the potatoes are tender and soft.

Transfer to food processor and puree.

Reheat and season to taste.

Stir in the cream.

Ladle soup into serving dishes.

Add buttered croutons (recipe follows).

Garnish with chives.

Serve hot.

Buttered Croutons

Ingredients (6 servings)

1 loaf day-old Italian bread

3 tablespoons butter

Instructions

Cut the bread into ¾ inch cubes.

Melt butter on medium high heat in sauté pan.

Add bread cubes and toss them in butter until lightly coated.

Spread the bread cubes out in a single layer in sauté pan.

Toast until golden brown on down side.

Flip and toast until entirely toasted on all sides.

Remove from heat.

Add to soup (recipe above).

Crepes filled with Ricotta Cheese and Spinach in Pink Sauce

Crepes filled with Ricotta Cheese and Spinach

Ingredients (8 servings)

8 ounces spinach

¼ cup pine nuts

1 tablespoon olive oil

1 onion

1 garlic clove, crushed

1½ cups fresh ricotta cheese

1 pinch ground nutmeg

8 fresh made crepes (recipe follows)

1½ cups tomato puree

1 cup coarsely grated cheddar

salt

fresh ground black pepper

Instructions

Preheat oven to 350°F.

Wash spinach and trim ends.

Chop onion fine.

Place spinach in large saucepan on medium heat.

Cover and cook 3-4 minutes, stirring occasionally.

Drain well and set aside 5 minutes until cooled.

Squeeze out moisture from spinach and chop coarsely.

Place chopped spinach in large bowl.

Toast pine nuts 2 minutes in a medium sauté pan on high heat.

Add toasted pine nuts to the spinach.

Add olive oil to sauté pan and heat on medium heat.

Add onion and garlic and sauté5 minutes, stirring occasionally.

Transfer onion and garlic to the bowl of spinach.

Add ricotta and nutmeg.

Stir until well mixed.

Season crepe filling to taste with salt and pepper.

Place crepe on clean work surface.

Divide spinach filling into 8 equal portions.

Spoon 1 portion of spinach filling into the center of the crepe.

Roll up tight to enclose filling.

Place filled crepe in large baking dish.

Repeat with remainder of crepes and filling to form rows of crepes in the baking dish.

Spoon tomato puree over crepes.

Sprinkle with cheddar cheese.

Bake in oven for 20 minutes.

Crepes are done when cheese melts and crepes are heated throughout.

Crepes

Ingredients (8 servings)

2 eggs

½ cup milk

½ cup water

1 cup all-purpose flour

¼ teaspoon salt

2 tablespoons butter, melted

Instructions

Whisk eggs in large bowl.

Slowly add milk and water as you stir.

Stir until combined.

Sift in flour.

Add salt and butter.

Beat until smooth.

Lightly oil frying pan.

Heat on medium high.

Pour ¼ cup batter into pan and swish to coat evenly.

Cook the crepe for 2 minutes.

When bottom is light brown, turn and cook other side.

Serve.

Pink Cream Sauce

Ingredients

½ pound bacon

½ teaspoon red pepper flakes

½ cup diced onion

3 garlic cloves, minced

28 ounces plum tomatoes, coarsely chopped

1½ cup heavy cream

½ teaspoon salt

3 tablespoons fresh minced parsley

Parmesan cheese

Instructions

Place bacon, pepper, onion and garlic in large skillet.

Cook 7 minutes on medium.

When onion is tender and bacon is done, add tomatoes, cream and salt.

Simmer 15 minutes until slightly thickened.

Add Parmesan cheese to taste.

Garnish with parsley.

Serve over stuffed crepes (recipe above).

Risotto with Green Apple and Champagne

Ingredients (4 servings)

2½ cups short grained rice

½ cup warm champagne

1 quart beef broth

¼ cup unsalted butter

½ small onion,

1 cup freshly grated Parmesan cheese

½ pound green apples

lemon juice

½ cup heavy cream

salt

fresh ground black pepper

Instructions

Bring beef broth to a simmer.

Peel, core, and cut apples into shavings.

Peel and finely chop onion.

Melt half the butter in a large sauté pan.

Slowly sauté the onion until it turns golden.

Add shaved apples.

Sprinkle apples with lemon juice.

Heat remaining butter in a large pot.

Add rice when butter starts to bubble.

Cook, stirring frequently, until rice grains turn translucent.

Add warmed champagne and stir until evaporated.

Add the apple mixture and begin adding broth.

Add broth one ladleful at a time as it is absorbed into the rice.

Cook the risotto, stirring often, until the rice reaches the al dente stage

Season to taste with salt and pepper.

Remove from heat, stir in the heavy cream, and cover 2 minutes.

Place the apple risotto in serving dishes.

Dust with grated cheese.

Serve immediately.

Broiled Marinated Lobster and Rice Creole

Broiled Marinated Lobster

Ingredients (4 servings)

4 lobster tails

2 tablespoons olive oil

2 garlic cloves, minced

½ teaspoon chili paste

½ cup fresh basil, chopped

1 teaspoon sea salt

fresh ground black pepper

1 large freezer bag

Instructions

Remove and discard shells from lobster tails.

Cut each lobster tail in half along its length.

Remove and discard intestines.

Combine olive oil, garlic, basil, chili paste, salt and pepper in large freezer bag.

Seal the halved lobster tails in the freezer bag with the marinade.

Shake bag until each lobster tail is thoroughly coated.

Refrigerate 2½ hours.

Broil the tails until white and opaque.

Rice Creole

Ingredients

2 quarts water

2 cups Basmati rice

4 fresh Bay leaves

2 tablespoons salt

2 tablespoons unsalted butter

Instructions

Preheat oven to 400°F

Place water in large pot with the Bay leaves.

Bring to a boil.

Add salt.

Add rice and stir well when it comes back to a boil.

Partially cover and cook 10-12 minutes until al dente.

Drain rice.

Pluck out and discard Bay leaves.

Transfer rice to baking dish.

Place butter on top of rice.

Bake in oven for 15 minutes.

Serve hot.

Beef Medallions on Bread Croutons and Mushroom Sauce

Beef Medallions & Mushroom Sauce

Ingredients (12 servings)

1½ pounds beef tenderloin

4 tablespoons butter

4 garlic cloves, chopped

2/3 cup shallots, chopped

1 teaspoon dried thyme

1 tablespoon all-purpose flour

2 cups beef broth

2 cups dry red wine

1 cup sliced mushrooms

salt

fresh ground black pepper

Instructions

Cut tenderloin crosswise into 12 equal rounds.

Pound beef rounds until they form flat ¼ -inch thick medallions.

Season lightly with salt and pepper.

Melt 2 tablespoons butter in large skillet on medium-high heat.

Sauté medallions 2 minutes until browned

Turn medallions over and sauté 2 more minutes to brown other side.

Set aside medallions.

Melt 2 tablespoons butter in same skillet.

Add mushrooms, garlic, shallots and thyme.

Sauté 3 minutes until tender.

Add flour.

Stir 1 minute.

Add broth and wine.

Boil 12 minutes, stirring occasionally, until sauce thickens and reduces to 1¼ cups.

Return medallions to skillet.

Heat 1 minute until medallions are hot throughout.

Top the croutons (recipe follows) with the beef medallions.

Spoon sauce equally over medalions.

Bread Croutons

Ingredients (12 servings)

2 loaves Italian bread

¼ cup olive oil

2 garlic cloves

Instructions

Preheat broiler.

Cut bread diagonally into ½ -inch slices.

Brush both sides of each slice lightly with olive oil.

Place bread on baking sheet.

Broil the slices 3 inches from the heat until toasted golden brown.

Turn over and broil other side.

Rub top of each crouton with the peeled garlic.

Transfer to serving plates and top with beef medallions (recipe above)

Baked Lamb Loin Aromatized with Herbs and Mint Sauce

Ingredients (6 servings)

2 pounds lamb loin

2 tablespoons salt

3 tablespoons extra virgin olive oil

3 tablespoons unsalted butter

3 tablespoons rosemary leaves

3 tablespoons marjoram leaves

¼ cup parsley

¼ cup mint leaves

3 tablespoons chopped chives

1 tablespoon ground fennel

1 tablespoon fresh grated orange zest

1 teaspoon ground cumin

Instructions

Preheat oven to 400°F

Trim lamb loin of any skin and fat.

Cut the lamb loin into 6 equal portions.

Sauté the portions in a skillet on medium high heat.

When golden brown all over, place lamb on rack and let cool.

Bring a pot of salted water to a boil.

Blanch fresh herbs in boiling water.

Transfer herbs to an ice bath. Wring herbs dry.

Chop herbs well and blend with olive oil and dried spices.

Warm butter, salt and orange zest together.

Whisk the herb infused oil and butter mixture together.

Pour mix over the lamb portions and place in preheated oven.

Cook 20 minutes for medium rare, longer or shorter to order.

Pojarsky Vegetables Served with Cheese Fondue

Pojarsky vegetables

Ingredients

1 onion, chopped

2 tablespoons chopped parsley

6 tablespoons milk

¾ cup breadcrumbs

2 eggs

2 garlic cloves, minced

1 assortment vegetables such as broccoli, asparagus, brussel sprouts, potato wedges, sweet potato wedges, parsnip wedges green beans, snow peas, snap peas, bell pepper slices, celery sticks, or mushrooms according to season

salt

fresh ground black pepper

Instructions

Combine onion, parsley, milk, breadcrumbs, eggs, garlic, salt and pepper in a large bowl.

Add additional breadcrumbs until batter is thick.

Refrigerate 2 hours.

Preheat oven to 375 degrees F.

Toss vegetables in batter until well coated.

Cook in oven 30 minutes.

Serve with Cheese Fondue (recipe follows)

Cheese Fondue

Ingredients

1 clove garlic, minced

½ pound Gruyère cheese

½ pound Emmental cheese

3 tablespoons unbleached all-purpose flour

1¾ cups dry white wine

¼ teaspoon fresh grated nutmeg

1 splash kirsch

Instructions

Toss the cheese with the flour.

Apply and rub the peeled garlic to the inside of a medium saucepan.

Place pan on medium heat

Add white wine and bring to a simmer.

Add cheese mix, little by little.

Stir nutmeg in.

Continue to stir on low heat until smoothed.

Add kirsch when cheese is melted and bubbly.

Continue to stir until fondue only bubbles a little.

Transfer to a fondue pot for dipping.

Serve with Pojarsky Vegetables (recipe above)

Potatoes Croquettes

Ingredients (6 servings)

2½ pounds russet potatoes

½ pound mozzarella cheese

¼ cup grated parmesan

1 tablespoon onion salt

¼ cup fresh parsley, chopped fine

3 large eggs

1 cup breadcrumbs

2½ cups olive oil

salt

½ teaspoon pepper

Instructions

Peel and quarter potatoes.

Simmer 15 minutes in a large pot of salted water.

Drain potatoes when tender.

Let cool 45 minutes.

Chop mozzarella into small pieces.

Mash potatoes well.

Stir in cheeses, onion salt, parsley, pepper, and salt to taste.

Stir in 1 egg.

Shape ¼ cup of mixture into a croquette.

Repeat until all the mixture is made into croquettes..

Lightly beat last 2 eggs in a shallow bowl.

Sprinkle breadcrumbs in a second bowl.

One at a time, dip croquettes into beaten eggs and roll in breadcrumbs until coated.

Heat oil in skillet on medium-high heat until oil shimmers.

Fry croquettes 5 minutes, turning occasionally.

When golden brown drain on paper towels.

Serve hot.

Spanish Salad

Ingredients (6 servings)

1 head iceberg lettuce

3 carrots, grated

12 mushrooms

12 cherry tomatoes, halved

1½ cups green beans

4 ounces salami, sliced

4 ounces chorizo, sliced

½ onion cut into rings

12 spears white asparagus

1 cup green olives

extra virgin olive oil

balsamic vinegar

salt

Instructions

Wash and chop the lettuce.

Place chopped lettuce in the center of a large platter.

Ring the rim of the platter with tomato halves.

Add onion rings in the center.

Arrange asparagus like wheel spokes with tips radiating outwards from center.

Add carrots, mushrooms, green beans, salami and chorizo to the center.

Sprinkle olives around platter edge.

Add salt and balsamic vinegar to taste.

Drizzle well with olive oil.

Serve immediately.

Baked Alaska alla Flamme

Ingredients (Serves 6)

1 quart ice cream

3 large eggs

1 cup water

1/3 cup sugar

½ cup flour

½ teaspoon almond extract

1/8 teaspoon cream of tartar

1/8 teaspoon salt

2 teaspoons cornstarch

4 egg whites

¾ cup powdered sugar

2 ounces Cognac

Instructions

Soften ice cream at room temperature for 1 hour.

Bring water to a simmer over low heat in a small sauce pan.

Preheat oven to 425 degrees.

Beat eggs and sugar and almond extract in a small steel mixing bowl over simmering water (double boiler), until the temperature reaches 110-120 degrees.

Remove from heat and continue beating until light and creamy and cooled.

Add flour and cornstarch.

Fold gently. Do not over mix.

Place a sheet of wax paper on a greased baking pan.

Spread the sponge base mixture thinly over the wax paper forming a rectangle.

Bake in oven for 5 minutes.

Remove from oven and let cool.

Remove cake from wax paper.

Cover the bottom and sides of your choice of mold with pieces of cake.

Put the softened ice cream on top of the cake to fill the mold.

Cover the top with more cake.

Freeze for 3 hours.

Beat egg whites, cream of tartar, salt and powdered sugar to a stiff meringue.

Place meringue in a piping bag.

Preheat oven to 425 degrees.

Remove frozen ice cream cake from mold and place on baking tray.

Pipe the meringue over top and sides of the cake.

Sculpture meringue as desired.

Bake in the oven for 4 minutes.

Cake is done when meringue edges are browned.

The meringue surface should be baked, while the ice cream inside remains frozen.

Pour the Cognac over the meringue surface.

Ignite with a long tapered match.

Serve flaming.

Small Assorted Pastries

Apple Turnovers

Ingredients

1 large Granny Smith apple

3 tablespoons raisins

2 tablespoons chopped walnuts

¼ cup sugar

¼ teaspoon cinnamon

½ teaspoon corn starch

¼ cup apple sauce

1/8 teaspoon vanilla

2½ cups all-purpose flour

½ teaspoon salt

1 cup butter

2 tablespoons butter, cut into bits

1 large egg

1 teaspoon milk

Instructions

Mix flour and salt in a small bowl.

With a large-tined fork blend chilled butter into the flour until coarse and sandy.

A few small pellets of butter will still be visible.

Sprinkle water over the mixture.

Toss gently until a stable ball of dough forms.

Divide the dough and flatten into sheets.

Wrap in plastic and chill several hours.

Pre-heat oven to 400°F

Peel, core and dice apple into ¼ -inch cubes.

Mix apples, raisins, walnuts, sugar, cinnamon and corn starch in a medium bowl.

Mix until fruit and nuts are well coated.

Mix in apple sauce and vanilla.

Unfold the chilled pastry on a lightly floured surface.

Roll out dough to a rough 16x11 inch rectangle.

Trim edges to 15x10 inches.

Cut into six 5x5-inch squares.

Divide apple mixture equally between the squares. Leave a 1-inch border.

Lightly beat egg.

Mix the beaten egg with a teaspoon of milk in a small bowl.

Brush onto the pastry border.

Fold each pastry into a triangle turned over the apple filling.

Crimp edges with fork.

Brush the tops of the pastries with the beaten egg.

Nick 3 small vents in the top of each turnover.

Put the turnovers on a large buttered baking sheet.

Place the pastries in the oven on a low oven rack

Bake 20 minutes.

Turnovers are done when puffed and golden.

Let turnovers cool a little.

Serve warm

Pasta Ciotti

Ingredients (Dough)

2 cups unbleached all-purpose flour

½ cup sugar

¾ teaspoon baking powder

1/8 teaspoon salt

½ cup vegetable shortening

¼ cup milk

¾ teaspoon vanilla extract

1 large egg, well beaten

Ingredients (Pastries)

3 tablespoons cornstarch

2/3 cup sugar

1½ cups milk

1½ tablespoons unsalted butter

1 large egg yolk, lightly beaten

1 teaspoon almond extract

1 large egg

1 teaspoon milk

Instructions

Sift flour, sugar, baking powder, and salt into a large bowl.
Blend in the shortening until the mix resembles coarse
cornmeal.

Add milk, vanilla, and egg.

Mix by hand into a smooth ball of dough.

Wrap the dough in plastic wrap and set aside.

Whisk cornstarch and sugar in a medium saucepan until blended smooth.

Slowly whisk in milk.

Add butter and cook on medium heat.

Stir continuously until thickened.

Remove from heat.

Stir in lightly beaten egg yolk and almond extract.

Set custard aside.

Divide dough in two pieces.

On a lightly floured surface, roll one piece into an 11-inch circle,.

With a 3-inch fluted biscuit cutter, cut circles of dough.

Press cut dough into the bottom and sides of 3x1¼ -inch tart pans.

Roll dough scraps and cut circles until you have 12 tart shells.

Place tart pans on a cookie sheet.

Spoon 2 tablespoons of filling into each tart shell.

Roll out the second piece of dough and cut out 3-inch circles.

Place cut circles as lids over each tart.

Pinch the edges closed.

Lightly beat egg.

Mix the beaten egg with a teaspoon of milk in a small bowl.

Brush the top of each tart with the beaten egg wash.

Refrigerate tarts 30 minutes.

Preheat oven to 425 degrees F.

Bake tarts on middle rack 12 minutes.

Tarts are done when tops are golden brown.

Remove to racks and let cool.

Carefully remove the tarts from the pans.

Refrigerate until served.

Petits Pains au Chocolat

Ingredients

2½ cups all-purpose flour

½ teaspoon salt

1 cup butter

2 tablespoons butter, cut into bits

2 3.5-ounce bars bittersweet Swiss dark chocolate

2 3.5-ounce bars Swiss milk chocolate

¼ cup sugar

1 large egg

1 tablespoon water

Instructions

Mix flour and salt in a small bowl.

With a large-tined fork blend chilled butter into the flour until coarse and sandy.

A few small pellets of butter will still be visible.

Sprinkle water over the mixture.

Toss gently until a stable ball of dough forms.

Divide the dough and flatten into sheets.

Wrap in plastic and chill several hours.

Pre-heat oven to 400°F

Unfold the chilled pastry on a lightly floured surface.

Roll out dough to a rough 16x11 inch rectangle.

Trim edges to 15x10 inches.

Cut into twenty-four 2½x2½-inch squares.

Line a baking sheet with parchment paper.

Lightly beat egg.

Mix the beaten egg with a tablespoon of water in a small bowl.

Brush beaten egg glaze on top of each pastry square.

Cut each chocolate bar into six 2x¾-inch pieces.

Place one piece of chocolate on edge of a pastry square.

Roll tightly, wrapping chocolate in dough.

Place rolled up pastry on baking sheet with seam on bottom.

Repeat until all pastry squares and chocolate are used.

Brush remaining egg glaze over the pastry rolls.

Sprinkle lightly with sugar.

Place the pastries in the oven on a low oven rack

Bake 15 minutes.

Pastries are done when golden brown.

Let pastries cool a little.

Serve warm.

Tropical Ice Cream Cup - Vanilla Ice cream with Rum, Coconut, Raisins and Whipped Cream

Ingredients (6 servings)

½ cup raisins

2 tablespoons rum

½ cup shredded coconut

3 cups coconut milk

1 cup + 6 tablespoons sugar

2 tablespoons tapioca flour

1 pinch salt

1 teaspoon vanilla extract

1 teaspoon apple cider vinegar

2 cups heavy cream

Instructions

Preheat oven to 300°F.

Place rum in a small saucepan on medium heat.

Mix in raisins and stir well.

Remove from heat and allow raisins to absorb the warm rum 15 minutes.

Sprinkle shredded coconut evenly on a large baking sheet.

Bake 20 minutes.

Coconut turns golden when done.

Put coconut milk in a medium saucepan on medium heat.

Add 1 cup + 2 tablespoons sugar, tapioca flour, salt and toasted coconut.

Bring to a simmer.

Remove from heat while whisking continuously.

Transfer to a covered bowl and refrigerate 3 hours.

Stir in vanilla extract and apple cider vinegar.

Beat with a mixer for 5 minutes.

Stir in the rum soaked raisins and with any unabsorbed rum.

Mix in an ice cream maker for 30 minutes.

Transfer to a covered container and freezer 3 hours.

Chill a metal mixing bowl and metal whisk in the freezer for 15 minutes.

Place remaining 4 tablespoons sugar in chilled bowl and add the heavy cream.

Whisk just until the whipped cream reaches stiff peaks.

Scoop ice cream into serving dishes.

Top with whipped cream.

Serve immediately.

CHAPTER FOUR

President's Dinner

All the signs pointed towards Antigua. The island had warm steady winds, a complex coastline of safe harbors, and a protective, nearly unbroken wall of coral reef. It would make a perfect place to hide a fleet. And so in 1784 the legendary Admiral Horatio Nelson sailed to Antigua and established Great Britain's most important Caribbean base. Little did he know that over 200 years later the same unique characteristics that attracted the Royal Navy would transform

Antigua and Barbuda into one of the Caribbean's premier tourist destinations.

The signs are still there, they just point to different things. The Trade Winds that once blew British men-of-war safely into English Harbor now fuel one of the world's foremost maritime events, Sailing Week. The expansive, winding coastline that made Antigua difficult for outsiders to navigate is where today's trekkers encounter a tremendous wealth of secluded, powdery soft beaches. The coral reefs, once the bane of marauding enemy ships, now attract snorkelers and scuba divers from all over the world. And the fascinating little island of Barbuda, once a scavenger's paradise because so many ships wrecked on its reefs, is now home to one of the region's most significant bird sanctuaries.

The luxurious 965-foot Norwegian Dawn carrying over 2,200 passengers launched in December of 2002 from New York City for the Caribbean. Since then, she's taken travelers to the tropical paradise, with its clear turquoise waters, fine pink sands, and palm trees swaying in the warm breeze. The relaxing tempo of reggae music and the sultry sounds of steel drums float through the sweetly scented air as our reader sips a creamy pina colada and lounges in a chaise on the sun deck as day 4 visits the sun-drenched island of Antigua.

NCL's Freestyle Cruising program lets diners enjoy any of the ten restaurants at any time, with no assigned seating or set hours for dinner. In the main restaurant, Impressions, reminiscent of Europe's grand hotels with Impressionist artwork evoking images of early 20th century Paris gracing its walls, the President's Dinner features meals served at the White House for special visitors, and presidents' and first ladies' favorite dishes, such as President Ford's favorite appetizer, Smoked Norwegian Salmon Terrine with Red Salmon Caviar Sauce, Nancy Reagan's light and exotic Cold Curry Soup with Sesame Seed Twist, and a favorite main course of President Carter: Sautéed Supreme of Chicken with Dry Sack Sherry. The only problem with this menu is deciding which exotic recipe to try first.

THE PRESIDENT'S DINNER

COLD APPETIZERS

President Ford's Smoked Norwegian Salmon Terrine
with Red Salmon Caviar Sauce
*This appetizer was one of the more sophisticated first
courses created for President Ford.
He always came to the table with a healthy appetite after
swimming
in the White House outdoor pool, rain or shine.*

Lady Diana's Asparagus Mousse in a Tomato Cup with
Baby Shrimps
*When Prince Charles and Princess Diana came for dinner
at the White House,
this mousse was served. She liked it so much it was
named after her.*

Cooking Light Ambrosia
Fresh Fruit Cocktail with Coconut Flakes and Dark Rum

HOT APPETIZER

President Reagan's *Gruyère Cheese Crepes Fondue*
*The signature appetizer during the Reagan
administration.
The first family liked it very much and requested that it be
served often*

THE SOUP KETTLE

Lady Bird Johnson's Beef Consommé with White House
Garden Vegetables
*The Johnson family liked soups and entrées featuring
beef.
President Johnson was also fond of a great variety of
fresh and colorful vegetables.*

President Nixon's North Atlantic Crab Soup with French Bread Croutons

In the First Family kitchen, Mr. Nixon spoke about fine food. He loved rich food but wanted to stay slim and trim. Desserts were only served when the first family entertained guests.

Nancy Reagan's Cold Curry Soup with Sesame Seed Twist

Curry soup was Mrs. Reagan's favorite. Nancy Reagan preferred light and exotic foods with equal emphasis on taste and artistic appearance.

FRESH FROM THE GARDEN

Jacqueline Kennedy's Garden Salad with Olive Oil Dressing and Melba Toast

In 1973 President Nixon invited Mrs. Kennedy, son John and daughter Caroline to the White House for dinner and to view Jacqueline Kennedy's First Lady portrait. She complimented this salad that was named after her.

Betty Ford's Hearts of Palm-and-Cucumber Salad with Red Bell Pepper Dressing

1976 was the bicentennial year celebration of the United States and a busy year at the White House. Kings and queens, prime ministers and presidents from around the world came to honor our country. Mrs. Ford understood the workload the kitchen was facing as it prepared all those state dinners. She especially loved this salad, served for lunch and dinner.

MAIN COURSES

Nancy Reagan's Poached Sea Bass in Champagne-and-Saffron Sauce

Parisienne Potatoes, Glazed Cherry Tomatoes and asparagus Spears
For this dish Mrs. Reagan told the chefs, "Put your heads together and
come up with a different way of serving Sea Bass."
This recipe was the answer and she liked it very much.

President Carter's Sautéed Supreme of Chicken with Dry Sack Sherry with Red and Green Peppers and Tomato Rice Pilaf
On the Carter family table there were other chicken dishes besides
Southern Fried Chicken, including this one. President Carter often
came into the kitchen to say, "Good supper!"

President Reagan's Roast Rack of Lamb California Rosé-Wine Shallots Sauce, Princess Potatoes and Fennel Gratinée
Nancy Reagan carefully studied both the family and official menus
so as to serve healthy food. Roast lamb was one of their favorites.
The president asked for his lamb to be served "rosé,"
meaning pink.

President Johnson's Grilled Butterflied Tenderloin of Beef
With Crimini Mushrooms served with Honey-Glazed Baby Carrots and New Red Bliss Potatoes
This entrée could be prepared in a short time, just as the President liked it. Dinner had to be ready upon his arrival so that his precious time was not wasted over food.

VEGETARIAN ENTREE
Cooking Light Spinach Lasagna

ASSORTMENT OF AMERICAN

CHEESES

DESSERTS

President Reagan's Floating Island with Cointreau Sauce
President Reagan was very fond of this dessert! When he was in the hospital recovering from his gunshot wound, he requested he be sent "a goodly portion of floating islands."

President Johnson's Chocolate Mousse with Toasted Hazelnuts-and-Brandy Sauce
*President Johnson loved this one. His doctor was always after him
to restrict his caloric intake, which was very hard to do.*

President Ford's Plum Torte Chantilly
*Plums and cherries are familiar fruits to someone raised in the state of Michigan.
President Ford felt right at home with this plum torte.*

FROM THE ICE CREAM PARLOR
Choice of Ice Creams and Sherberts

The President's Dinner Recipes

President Ford's Smoked Norwegian Salmon Terrine with Red Salmon Caviar Sauce

Smoked Norwegian Salmon Terrine

Ingredients (6 servings)

1 pound sliced smoked Norwegian salmon

2 cups cream cheese

¼ cup cream

1 tablespoon lemon zest

2 tablespoons lemon juice

1/3 cup fresh dill, finely chopped

2 tablespoons capers

fresh ground black pepper

Instructions

Place cream cheese, cream, lemon zest, lemon juice, dill and capers in a food processor.

Season to taste with pepper and combine.

Butter a 6 cup terrine pan.

Line base and sides with plastic wrap overhanging two inches at ends.

Layer enough smoked salmon to cover bottom of pan.

Layer 1/3 cup cream cheese mixture equally over salmon.

Repeat layering process until all the salmon is used.

The top layer should be salmon.

Fold plastic wrap over salmon, pressing down gently.

Refrigerate overnight.

Before serving, turn onto a platter and remove wrap.

Trim ends and cut into slices.

Drizzle with red salmon caviar sauce (recipe follows). Serve.

Red Salmon Caviar Sauce

Ingredients

1 cup sour cream

8 ounces crème fraiche

½ cup mayonnaise

4 tablespoons fresh dill, chopped

1 pinch white pepper

3½ ounces red salmon caviar

Instructions

Combine sour cream, creme fraiche, mayonnaise, dill, and white pepper in a bowl. Stir well.

Carefully mix in caviar.

Cover and refrigerate 1 hour.

Drizzle over salmon terrine (recipe above).

Lady Diana's Asparagus Mousse in a Tomato Cup

Ingredients (4 servings)

4 large tomatoes

1 pound asparagus, trimmed and peeled

2 large eggs, separated

¼ teaspoon dried tarragon

Pinch of freshly grated nutmeg

½ teaspoon salt

Freshly ground white pepper

Lemon zest curls

Instructions

Preheat the oven to 350°F.

Steam the asparagus until tender.

Drain and transfer to absorbent paper.

Pat the stalks dry and reserve 4 tips for garnish.

Slice off the tomato tops.

With a sharp knife, gently cut around the insides.

Scoop out the seeds and place the tomato shell cups in a

baking dish.

Cut asparagus into 1-inch lengths.

Purée asparagus in food processor until smooth.

Blend in egg yolks, one by one.

Blend in tarragon, nutmeg, salt and pepper to taste.

Whisk egg whites in a large mixing bowl until they reach soft peaks.

Fold in the asparagus purée.

Pour mixture into the prepared tomato cups and loosely cover each with aluminum foil.

Pour an inch of boiling water into baking dish.

Bake 30 minutes.

When done, a slender knife blade inserted in the center comes out clean.

Garnish with asparagus tips and lemon curls.

Serve hot.

Fresh Fruit Cocktail with Coconut Flakes and Dark Rum

Ingredients (6 servings)

2 mangoes (peeled and cubed)

2 bananas (peeled and sliced)

1 cup fresh pineapple (peeled and cubed)

2 oranges (peeled and segmented)

1 kiwi fruit (peeled and sliced)

¼ cup dark rum

½ cup coconut flakes

Instructions

Set aside coconut flakes.

Mix all the other fruit together in a large glass bowl.

Pour rum over the fruit and mix well.

Refrigerate until chilled.

Toast coconut flakes 2 minutes in a medium sauté pan on high heat.

Coconut is done when toasted golden.

Transfer chilled fruit to tall cocktail glasses.

Sprinkle toasted coconut over the fruit cocktails and serve.

President Reagan's Gruyère Cheese Crepes Fondue

Gruyère Cheese Crepes

Ingredients (4 servings)

1 cup milk

1 egg

½ cup plus 1 tablespoon all-purpose flour

½ teaspoon canola oil

½ teaspoon salt

8 teaspoons unsalted butter

12 ounces Gruyère cheese, thinly sliced

Fresh ground black pepper

Instructions

Combine milk, egg, flour, canola oil and salt in a food processor.

Blend 1 minute until smooth.

Cover and refrigerate 3 hours.

Melt 1 teaspoon of butter in a crepe pan on medium heat.

Swirl pan to coat evenly.

Raise pan on a slight tilt.

Pour 2 tablespoons of crepe batter into the center.

Angle the pan to spread the batter out to the edges.

Return the pan to the heat and cook 2 minutes.

Crepe is ready to turn when golden underneath.

Flip with a spatula and cook other side 2 minutes until golden.

Lay crepe flat on a plate and cover.

Repeat process until batter is used up in 8 cooked crepes.

Lay one crepe flat on a clean work surface.

Arrange 1½ ounces cheese on the crepe.

Add salt and pepper to taste.

Fold the crepe into quarters.

Repeat until all crepes and cheese are used.

Lightly butter the crepe pan and put on medium heat.

Place crepes in pan and cook 2 minutes each side until cheese startss to melt.

Drizzle with fondue sauce (recipe follows)

Serve immediately.

Cheese Fondue Sauce

Ingredients (4 servings)

1 cup Riesling wine

1¼ cups Gruyère cheese, shredded

1 cup Emmentaler cheese, shredded

1½ tablespoons cornstarch

1 garlic clove

1/8 teaspoon nutmeg

salt

Instructions

Rub fondue pot with peeled garlic clove.

Chop clove in half and mince.

Add a sprinkling of salt.

Mash into a paste.

Bring wine to a simmer.

Toss shredded cheeses with cornstarch.

Add cheese to wine in batches, stirring continuously until smooth.

Add garlic paste and nutmeg.

Stir well.

Spoon sauce over crepes (recipe above) before serving.

Lady Bird Johnson's Beef Consommé with Garden Vegetables

Ingredients (6 servings)

½ pound beef shoulder

3 pints beef stock (recipe follows)

¼ pint water

1 ounce carrots

1 ounce celery

1 ounce leeks

1 ounce onion

2 egg whites

1 tablespoon peppercorns

1 sachet Bouquet Garni, (parsley, thyme, oregano, marjoram, bay and basil)

1 level teaspoon salt.

2 tablespoons dry sherry

Instructions

Trim off fat and cut beef into thin slices.

Chop vegetables to a fine dice.

Combine beef stock, water, vegetables, beef, eggs whites, peppercorns, Bouquet Garni and salt in a large stockpot.

Bring to a boil, stirring constantly.

Reduce heat and let simmer 40 minutes without stirring.

Remove from heat.

Strain through a fine sieve lined with a double layer of cheesecloth.

Set aside vegetables and discard remaining contents of sieve.

Return Garden Vegetables and broth to pan.

Heat thoroughly.

Remove from heat and add sherry.

Serve hot.

Beef Stock

Ingredients (6 pints)

10 pounds beef shins, cut into strips

18 pints water

2 onions, halved.

1 large leek, halved

2 carrots

4 sticks celery

2 bay leaves

1 heaped teaspoon salt

¼ cup peppercorns

1 sprig thyme,

1 sprig parsley

Instructions

Preheat the oven to 325°F

Roughly chop vegetables.

Place vegetables on a baking sheet with beef strips.

Roast in oven until browned.

Transfer meat and vegetables to a large stock pot.

Add water, spices, peppercorns and salt.

Bring to a boil.

Skim, lower to simmer 8 hours.

Strain out the vegetables, bones and spices.

Strain into a new pan.

Cool overnight.

Gently lift hardened congealed fat from top of the stock with tongs.

Store and refrigerate until use.

President Nixon's North Atlantic Crab Soup with French Bread Croutons

North Atlantic Crab Soup

Ingredients

3 tablespoons butter

¼ cup sweet onion, chopped

1 stalk celery, trimmed and chopped fine

3 carrots, peeled and chopped

2 tablespoons flour

2 cups fish stock

1 teaspoon Old Bay® seasoning.

2 cups milk

2 cups heavy cream

1½ pounds of lump crab meat.

3 tablespoons sherry

1½ teaspoons salt

¼ teaspoon of pepper.

paprika and chopped parsley for garnish

Instructions

Melt butter in a stock pot.

Add onion, celery and carrots.

Sauté 5 minutes until tender.

Add flour to make a roux.

Add fish stock and Old Bay® seasoning.

Stir in milk and heavy cream.

Simmer until thickened.

Fold in crab meat.

Remove from heat.

Add sherry, salt and pepper.

Sprinkle with paprika and chopped parsley.

Serve hot.

Add French Bread Crouton (recipe follows)

French Bread Croutons

Ingredients

1 loaf French bread

5 tablespoons olive oil

1 tablespoon basil

1 tablespoon oregano

3 tablespoons minced garlic

Salt

Instructions

Preheat oven to 325°F.

Cut French bread into ½" cubes.

Heat herbs, garlic, and oil in a large sauté pan until fragrant

Add cubed bread and toss until coated with herbs.

Spread the bread cubes on a lightly buttered baking sheet.

Bake for 20 minutes

Croutons are ready when hard and golden brown.

Salt to taste.

Add to North Atlantic Crab Soup (recipe above)

Nancy Reagan's Cold Curry Soup with Sesame Seed Twist

Cold Curry Soup

Ingredients (6 servings)

¼ cup butter

1 medium onion, sliced

3 medium apples, peeled, cored and sliced (save 2 slices for garnish)

1 carrot, sliced

1 green pepper, seeded and finely chopped

1 celery stalk, trimmed and diced

2 cloves

1½ teaspoons curry powder

1 parsley sprig, minced

fresh ground black pepper

salt

1 pinch fresh grated nutmeg

6 cups chicken broth

1 cup whipping cream

whipped cream for garnish

chopped apple for garnish

Instructions

Melt butter in 3 quart pan on medium high heat.

Add onion, sauté until tender.

Add apple, carrot, green pepper and celery.

Sauté 10 minutes.

Vegetables are done when tender.

Stir in cloves, curry, parsley and nutmeg.

Add broth, season to taste with salt and pepper.

Reduce heat, cover and simmer 35 minutes.

Remove from heat, blend in whipping cream.

Transfer to food processor in batches, purée.

Pour into serving bowls, cover.

Refrigerate until chilled.

Garnish with cream and apple.

Serve Chilled with Sesame Seed Twist (recipe follows).

Sesame Seed Twist

Ingredients

4 cups whole wheat pastry flour

1 cup sesame flour

¾ cup soy flour

1 tablespoon baking powder

1 cup butter

¾ cup honey

4 eggs

2 teaspoons vanilla

1 tablespoon water

Sesame seeds

Instructions

Preheat oven to 350°F

Combine flours and baking powder, set aside.

Cream butter and honey together.

Add 3 eggs and vanilla.

Beat until light and frothy.

Mix flour and cream blends until barely combined.

Roll a heaped tablespoon of dough into a 6" string

Fold string in half and twist together twice.

Repeat process until all dough is used.

Whisk fourth egg with water in a small bowl.

Brush each pastry with egg mixture.

Sprinkle pastries liberally with sesame seeds.

Place cookie sheet.

Bake 20 minutes at 350°F.

Remove from oven and cool on a rack.

Serve with Cold Curry Soup (recipe above).

Jacqueline Kennedy's Garden Salad with Olive Oil Dressing and Melba Toast

Garden Salad with Olive Oil Dressing

Ingredients (4 servings)

5 cups mixed torn lettuce

1 cup radicchio, chopped

1 cup alfalfa sprouts

1 cup grated carrot

1 small red onion sliced into thin rings

8 cherry tomatoes, halved

24 thin cut slices cucumber

1 sprig fresh oregano

1 sprig fresh thyme

1 cup olive oil

¼ cup balsamic vinegar

salt and pepper to taste

Instructions

Mix lettuce, radicchio, alfalfa sprouts, carrots and onions in large bowl.

Add cherry tomatoes and cucumber slices.

Combine the oregano, thyme, oil, vinegar, salt and pepper in a glass bowl.

Divide the garden salad evenly onto four serving plates.

Drizzle dressing over the salads.

Serve with Melba Toast (recipe follows).

Melba Toast

Ingredients (4 servings)

1 tablespoon unsalted butter, melted

1/8 teaspoon dried dill

1/8 teaspoon dried thyme

4 slices of fresh baked white bread

Instructions

Preheat oven to 350°F

Mix melted butter, dill and thyme in a small bowl.

Add salt and pepper to taste.

Roll bread very thin with a rolling pin.

Trim off crusts.

Brush bread with the butter mixture both sides

Cut slice diagonally into triangles

Place the triangles on a baking sheet on the center rack of oven.

Bake 15 minutes, turning halfway through.

Toasts are done when browned and crisp.

Cool the toasts on a rack.

Serve with Garden Salad (recipe above)

Betty Ford's Hearts of Palm-and-Cucumber Salad with Red Bell Pepper Dressing

Hearts of Palm-and-Cucumber Salad

Ingredients (4 servings)

½ small red onion, sliced thin

2 tablespoons white balsamic vinegar

2 avocados, diced

2 teaspoons fresh squeezed lemon juice

1 seedless cucumber, peeled, sliced and slices halved

14 ounces hearts of palm, sliced

1 cup cherry tomatoes, halved

1 tablespoon olive oil

¾ teaspoon dried mint

1½ teaspoons dried oregano

1 teaspoon kosher salt

fresh ground black pepper

salt

Instructions

Combine onion and vinegar in a small bowl.

Set aside 5 minutes.

Place avocado in a large bowl and gently mix in lemon juice

Add cucumber, hearts of palm, tomatoes, onions and vinegar.

Drizzle in olive oil.

Add mint, oregano.

Salt and pepper to taste.

Stir gently to combine.

Serve with Red Bell Pepper Dressing (recipe below)

Red Bell Pepper Dressing

Ingredients

2 red bell peppers

2 yellow bell peppers

¾ cup red wine vinegar

1 cup extra virgin olive oil

1 teaspoon salt

Instructions

Preheat broiler with oven rack 6" from heat.

Line baking sheet with aluminum foil.

Cut peppers in half, top to bottom.

Remove stem, seeds, and ribs.

Place peppers cut-half-down on baking sheet.

Broil 5 minutes .

Peppers are done when skin blackens and blisters.

Place blackened peppers in bowl, and cover tightly in plastic wrap.

Let peppers steam as they cool.

After 20 minutes, remove skins from cooled peppers.

Discard skins.

Transfer the roast peppers to food processor.

Add red wine vinegar, olive oil, and salt.

Process mixture until smooth.

Serve with Hearts of Palm-and-Cucumber Salad (recipe above)

Nancy Reagan's Poached Sea Bass in Champagne and Saffron Sauce

Poached Sea Bass

Ingredients (8 servings)

1 quart water

2 cups dry white wine

1 large leek, split long ways and sliced thin across

1 large carrot, sliced thin

1 bay leaf

salt

fresh ground black pepper

8 sea bass fillets with skin

2 tablespoons fresh parsley, chopped

2 tablespoons fresh chives, chopped

Instructions

Set a large pan over high heat.

Combine water, wine, leek, carrot and bay leaf and bring to a boil.

Lower heat and simmer 10 minutes.

Season to taste with salt and pepper.

Carefully add the fish fillets, skin up.

Poach minutes at a slow simmer.

Fish is done when cooked through.

Drain fish fillets on paper towels.

Transfer fish to warm dinner plates.

Drizzle with Champagne and Saffron Sauce (recipe follows).

Sprinkle with parsley and chives.

Serve hot.

Champagne and Saffron Sauce

Ingredients

1 pinch saffron threads

4 tablespoons butter

4 tablespoons champagne

1¼ cups heavy cream

juice of half a lemon, fresh squeezed

salt

fresh ground black pepper

1 sprig flat leaf parsley for garnish

Instructions

Heat a large skillet on high heat.

Add saffron threads and toast briefly until aromatic.

Remove saffron from skillet and set aside.

Melt 2 tablespoons butter in pan.

Add toasted saffron, champagne and heavy cream.

Bring to a boil.

Lower heat and simmer 10 minutes.

Reduction will coat the back of a spoon when done.

Add lemon juice.

Season to taste with salt and pepper.

Garnish with parsley.

Serve with Poached Sea Bass (recipe above).

President Carter's Sautéed Supreme of Chicken with Dry Sack Sherry with Red and Green Peppers and Tomato Rice Pilaf

Sautéed Supreme of Chicken with Dry Sack Sherry with Red and Green Peppers

Ingredients (8 servings)

8 chicken breasts

1 pound white button mushrooms

2 red bell peppers

2 green bell pepper

2 tomatoes, peeled and cut in quarters

1 cup dry sack sherry

4 tablespoons butter

salt

fresh ground black pepper

fresh squeezed lemon juice

I sprig fresh parsley

Instructions

Season chicken with salt, pepper and lemon juice to taste.

Cut peppers in half, top to bottom.

Remove stem, seeds, and ribs.

Slice peppers and set-aside.

Melt butter in skillet on medium high heat.

Sauté chicken until golden brown.

Remove chicken from skillet, set aside.

Add mushrooms and red wine to same skillet.

Heat until wine reduces in half.

Return chicken breasts to skillet.

Cover skillet and lower heat to a simmer

Cook 10 minutes.

Add peppers and tomatoes.

Heat uncovered until thoroughly warmed.

Garnish with parsley.

Serve on a bed of Tomato Rice Pilaf (recipe below)

Tomato Rice Pilaf

Ingredients (8 servings)

3 cups chicken stock

2 onions, chopped

2 cloves garlic, minced

2 tablespoons extra virgin olive oil

2 pounds tomatoes, peeled, deseeded and chopped

½ teaspoon fresh ground cinnamon

3 cups basmati rice

2 teaspoons salt

4 teaspoons fresh ground black pepper

½ cup fresh basil, chopped

½ cup toasted pine nuts

Instructions

Heat chicken stock to low simmer in medium saucepan.

Heat oil on medium low heat in large skillet.

Add onions and garlic.

Sauté until tender.

Add tomatoes and cinnamon.

Cook 5 minutes on lowered heat.

Add rice, stir well and cook 5 minutes.

Add simmering chicken stock.

Stir until mixed.

Cover and cook on low heat.

Rice is cooked when tender and liquid is absorbed.

Remove from heat and let sit 5 minutes.

Stir in salt, pepper, basil and pine nuts.

Serve with Sautéed Supreme of Chicken (recipe above).

President Reagan's Roast Rack of Lamb, California Rosé Wine-Shallots Sauce, Princess Potatoes and Fennel Gratinée

Roast Rack of Lamb

Ingredients (6 servings)

2 racks of lamb, Frenched (2 pounds each)

4 teaspoons fresh chopped rosemary

2 teaspoons fresh chopped thyme

4 cloves garlic, minced

salt

fresh ground black pepper

4 tablespoons extra virgin olive oil

Instructions

Combine rosemary, thyme, and garlic to make a rubbing mixture.

Rub rib racks entirely with herb mixture.

Sprinkle with pepper.

Place rib racks in a heavy plastic bag.

Add olive oil and toss until lamb racks are thoroughly coated.

Squeeze air from bag and seal.

Refrigerate overnight to marinate.

Remove lamb racks from refrigerator 2 hours before cooking to let reach room temperature.

Preheat oven to 400°F.

Make sharp shallow cuts through the fat at 1" intervals.

Sprinkle all over with salt and pepper.

Place lamb racks bone side down in roasting pan.

Wrap exposed ribs in tin foil.

Place pan on center oven rack.

Roast 7 minutes at 400°F.

Reduce heat to 300°F.

Roast 12 minutes at 300°F.

Meat is done to President Reagan's preference for rosé when a meat thermometer reads 125°F in the thickest part of the meat. If your preference is for medium rare it should read 135°F.

Remove from oven and cover with tin foil.

Let stand 10 minutes.

Slice between ribs to cut into 2 or 3 lamb chops per guest.

Drizzle with California Rosé Wine-Shallots Sauce (recipe follows)

Serve with Princess Potatoes and Fennel Gratinée (recipes follow)

California Rosé Wine-Shallots Sauce

Ingredients (6 servings)

1½ ounces butter

1¼ cups sliced shallots

2 tablespoons minced garlic

1 cup California Rosé Wine

1 bay leaf

2 cups veal stock

1 ounce butter

Instructions

Heat ½ ounce butter in a medium saucepan on medium-low heat.

Add shallots and garlic.

Sauté 5 minutes.

Shallots and garlic are done when tender.

Add wine and bay leaf.

Bring to a boil.

Cook until reduced in half.

Add veal stock.

Cook 20 minutes.

Sauce in ready when reduced by 1¾ cups.

Remove from heat and discard bay leaf.

Whisk in remaining ounce of butter.

Drizzle over Roast Rack of Lamb (recipe above)

Princess Potatoes

Ingredients (6 servings)

1½ pounds potatoes

1 large egg, beaten

¼ cup melted butter

1 clove garlic, crushed

1 pinch dried dill

¾ teaspoon salt

¼ teaspoon fresh ground black pepper

1½ tablespoons grated Parmesan cheese

2½ tablespoons heavy cream

¼ teaspoon paprika

1 sprig fresh parsley

Instructions

Peel potatoes and cut into cubes.

Place cubes in a large stock pot of water.

Bring to a boil on medium-high heat.

Boil until tender.

Drain and return potatoes to stock pot.

Whip with an electric mixer.

Slowly mix in beaten egg, half of the butter, garlic, dill, grated cheese, heavy cream, salt and pepper.

Continue whipping until the smooth.

Test consistency and add more milk if needed.

Season to taste with salt and pepper.

Place whipped potatoes in a pastry bag fitted with a large star tip.

Grease a large, greased baking sheet and pipe whipped potatoes into 12 mounds.

Drizzle the rest of the butter over the potatoes.

Using a pastry brush, dab a little paprika paste lightly onto each potato mound.

Garnish with a sprinkling of dried parsley.

Preheat oven to 400°F

Bake 20 minutes.

Potatoes are done when golden brown at the edges.

Remove from oven and serve piping hot.

Fennel Gratinée

Ingredients (6 servings)

1 large shallot, minced

¾ cup red wine

2½ tablespoons unsalted butter

salt

fresh ground black pepper

3 tablespoons butter

¾ cup breadcrumbs

1 cup Pecorino Romano cheese

3 tablespoons fresh parsley, chopped

1½ teaspoons lemon zest

5 tablespoons olive oil

1 onion, halved and sliced ¼" thick

3 large garlic cloves, minced

5 fresh fennel bulbs, trimmed, cored and sliced ¼" thick

½ cup low-sodium chicken broth

1 tablespoon chopped fresh thyme

1½ teaspoons sea salt

Instructions

Lightly oil a baking dish.

Heat olive oil in large skillet on medium heat.

Sauté onion and garlic 5 minutes.

Onion and garlic are done when soft but not browned.

Add fennel and heat on medium-high heat.

Sauté fennel 15-20 minutes. Stir frequently.

Fennel is done when softened and starts to brown.

Stir in broth, 2 tablespoons parsley, thyme, sea salt and ½ teaspoon pepper.

Lower heat to medium-low and simmer 5 minutes.

After most of the broth absorbs transfer to baking dish.

Let stand at room temperature 1 hour before baking.

Preheat oven to 425 F.

Melt butter in large skillet on medium heat.

Add breadcrumbs and sauté 3 minutes.

Breadcrumbs are done when golden brown.

Remove from heat and let cool.

Stir cheese, 1 tablespoon parsley, and lemon zest into breadcrumbs.

Sprinkle breadcrumb mix over fennel.

Bake 20 minutes.

Dish is done when gratin is warmed through and topping is toasted golden brown.

Serve warm.

President Johnson's Grilled Butterflied Tenderloin of Beef with Crimini Mushrooms served with Honey Glazed Baby Carrots and New Red Bliss Potatoes

Grilled Butterflied Tenderloin of Beef

Ingredients (4 servings)

4 beef tenderloin steaks

1 tablespoon butter

1 teaspoon fresh garlic, finely chopped

½ teaspoon fresh ground black pepper

½ teaspoon chili powder

Instructions

Place a steak on a cutting board.

With a long sharp knife cut the steak horizontally at its midpoint to within a half inch of the other side.

Open the two flaps of meat without letting the pieces fall apart.

If done correctly steaks resemble butterfly wings.

Place the butterflied steak between two sheets of plastic wrap.

Beat with a meat mallet to an even thickness.

Repeat until all steaks are butterflied.

Heat a charcoal grill until coals are ash white.

Mix butter, garlic, pepper and chili powder in small bowl.

Brush steaks with butter mixture and place on grill.

Grill 15 minutes, turning once and brushing intermittently with butter mixture.

Crimini Mushrooms

Ingredients (4 servings)

1 tablespoon olive oil

8 ounces Crimini mushrooms

1/3 cup sherry

1 tablespoon Worcestershire sauce

2 teaspoons fresh thyme

Instructions

Heat olive oil in large skillet on medium-high heat.

Sauté mushrooms 4 minutes. Stir frequently.

Stir in wine, Worcestershire sauce, and thyme.

Simmer 3 minutes uncovered.

Spoon over steaks (recipe above).

Honey Glazed Baby Carrots

Ingredients (4 servings)

1 pound baby carrots

¾ teaspoon salt

2 tablespoons butter

2 tablespoons honey

1½ tablespoons brown sugar

2 teaspoons fresh squeezed lemon juice

fresh parsley, chopped for garnish

Instructions

Put carrots in a medium saucepan and cover with water.

Add salt and bring to boil.

Lower heat and cover.

Cook 15 minutes on medium-low heat.

Carrots are done when tender.

Drain and set aside.

Melt butter in saute pan on medium-low heat.

Add honey and brown sugar.

Stir until sugar is fully dissolved.

Mix in lemon juice and gently stir in carrots.

Stir carrots gently until well coated.

Continue heating and stirring until carrots are hot and glazed.

Garnish with chopped parsley.

Serve hot.

New Red Bliss Potatoes

Ingredients (4 servings)

1 pound new red bliss potatoes

1 head garlic

¼ cup extra virgin olive oil

salt

fresh ground black pepper

¼ cup water

¼ cup fresh grated parmesan cheese

2 tablespoons chopped parsley

Instructions

Preheat oven to 400°F

Scrub potatoes and cut into halves.

Peel garlic and break into cloves.

Combine potatoes, olive oil, garlic, salt and pepper in a large bowl.

Toss until well coated.

Arrange potatoes in a single layer inside roasting pan.

Sprinkle with water.

Roast 45 minutes.

Potatoes are done when tender and golden brown.

Toss potatoes and garlic in a serving bowl with cheese and parsley.

Serve hot.

Spinach Lasagna

Ingredients (12 servings)

2 large onions, sliced thin

4 sprigs thyme

6 zucchini, sliced

3 plum tomatoes, sliced very thin

20 lasagna noodles (recipe follows)

¼ cup pesto

1 pound ricotta cheese

½ cup grated Parmesan cheese

zest of 1 lemon

3 tablespoons fresh parsley, chopped fine

8 ounce mozzarella cheese, shredded

1 cup fresh breadcrumbs

½ cup olive oil

3 tablespoons butter

2 cups fresh spinach

salt

fresh ground black pepper

Instructions

Put spinach in a medium saucepan and cover with water.

Bring to boil.

Cook 5 minutes.

Drain, squeeze out excess moisture.

Chop spinach and set aside

Put 2 tablespoons olive oil and 1 tablespoon butter in large skillet on low heat.

Warm until butter melts.

Add onions and 2 sprigs of thyme leaves (leaves only).

Sauté 1 hour on low heat.

Onions are done when caramelized and sweet

Preheat oven to 300° F.

Toss zucchini slices with 4 tablespoons oil in a large bowl,

Season to taste with salt.

Arrange zucchini on large baking sheet.

Bake 40 minutes until tender.

Raise temperature to 400° F.

Bake 10 minutes until tops are browned.

Mix ricotta, parmesan, lemon zest and 2 tablespoons parsley in medium bowl.

Season to taste with salt and pepper.

Melt 2 tablespoons butter in a small pan on medium heat.

When foamed add remaining leaves of sprigs of thyme and 1 tablespoon parsley.

Remove from heat and whisk thoroughly.

Add breadcrumbs and toss to combine.

Set mixture aside.

Preheat oven to 350 °F.

Place one-third of onions, zucchini and tomatoes in a 9 x 13" baking dish.

Top with a layer of pasta noodles.

Brush one-third pesto evenly over pasta.

Spread one-third ricotta mix evenly on top.

Cover with a layer of one-third spinach

Top with one-third mozzarella.

Repeat process for two more layers.

Sprinkle breadcrumb mix evenly over top of lasagna.

Cover lasagna in aluminum foil.

Bake 20 minutes covered.

Remove aluminum and bake 40 minutes more.

Lasagna is done when bubbling.

Remove to cooling rack 15 minutes before serving.

Lasagna Noodles

Ingredients (20 lasagna noodles)

10 cups semolina flour

2½ teaspoon salt

2½ teaspoon basil

1½ teaspoon oregano

1½ teaspoon onion powder

1½ teaspoon garlic powder

4 cups warm water

Instructions

Mix flour, salt, basil, oregano, onion powder and garlic powder in a large bowl.

Pour water into flour and stir with wooden spoon.

Use hands to finish mixing dough.

Dough is ready when evenly mixed.

Sprinkle flour on a flat surface.

Knead dough 10 minutes.

Form dough into five equal balls.

Cover dough balls and let sit 15 minutes.

Quarter each dough ball so you have twenty equal size pieces.

Keep dough covered and moist as you roll noodles.

Take one piece and roll it into a strip a little over 3" wide by 6" long.

Trim with a knife to 3"x6" rectangular noodle.

Repeat until you have 20 noodles.

Boil a large pot of salted water.

Add noodles carefully one by one.

Cook 5 minutes.

Gently agitate noodles with a wooden spoon to keep from sticking.

Drain noodles and layer into lasagna (Recipe above).

Assortment Of American Cheeses

Ingredients

1 wedge Monterey Jack cheese

1 wedge Red Hawk cheese

1 wedge Maytag Blue cheese

1 wedge Humboldt Fog cheese

1 package water crackers

1 package butter crackers

1 package sesame crackers

1 package rice crackers

1 package cream crackers

2 small clusters seedless grapes

Instructions

At least half an hour before serving, arrange cheese wedges on cutting board

Provide a separate cheese knife for each cheese.

Place crackers on serving plates next to the cheese board.

Garnish with grapes.

Self-serve.

President Reagan's Floating Island with Cointreau Sauce

Meringue islands

Ingredients (6 servings)

½ cup egg whites

salt

2/3 cup sugar

6 thin lemon slices

12 ounces fresh raspberries

Instructions

Preheat oven to 350°F.

Butter six ¾-cup soufflé dishes.

Dust dishes with sugar.

Place on baking sheet.

Beat egg whites with pinch of salt in large bowl.

Beat to soft peaks.

Slowly beat in sugar and beat until stiff and glossy.

Split meringue equally between soufflé dishes, mounding slightly.

Bake 15 minutes.

Meringues are done when puffy and lightly browned on top.

Cool 20 minutes until room temperature

Divide Cointreau sauce (Recipe follows) equally into 6 shallow desert dishes.

Place meringues, top side up on top of sauce.

Garnish each meringue with a lemon slice.

Sprinkle raspberries equally over dishes.

Serve.

Cointreau sauce

Ingredients (6 servings)

½ cup water

½ cup caster sugar

1 lemon, zested

1 orange, zested

2 tablespoons Cointreau

Instructions

Place sugar and zests in ½ cup water in a saucepan.

Heat on medium heat.

Stir until sugar dissolves,

Bring to a boil, then lower heat to a low simmer.

Simmer for 3 minutes.

Remove heat and stir in Cointreau.

President Johnson's Chocolate Mousse with Toasted Hazelnuts-and-Brandy Sauce

Chocolate Mousse

Ingredients (6 servings)

½ cup heavy cream

4 egg yolks

¼ cup espresso, cooled

3 tablespoons sugar

1/8 teaspoon salt

6 ounces semisweet chocolate, chopped

2 egg whites

Instructions

Beat ½ cup heavy cream in medium bowl.

When stiff peaks form cover and chill.

Place yolks, espresso, salt, and 2 tablespoons sugar in large bowl.

Set bowl above a pot of simmering water without touching water.

Cook 1 minute, whisking continuously.

Mixture is done when lighter in color and nearly double in size.

Remove bowl from hot water.

Whisk in chocolate until melted and smooth.

Let cool to room temperature, whisking occasionally,.

Beat egg whites in a medium bowl until foamy.

Slowly beat in 1 tablespoon sugar.

Beat to firm peaks.

Fold egg whites into chocolate mixture in 2 additions.

Fold whipped cream into mixture.

Split mousse into six 4-ounce ramekins.

Chill 2 hours.

Mouse is ready to serve when cold and firm.

Brandy Sauce

Ingredients (6 servings)

¼ cup butter

½ cup brown sugar

2 tablespoons brandy

Instructions

Melt butter in small saucepan on medium-low heat.

Stir in brown sugar.

When sugar is fully dissolved remove from heat.

Stir in brandy.

Serve over chocolate mousse (recipe above).

Toasted Hazelnuts

Ingredients (6 servings)

2 cups hazlenuts

Instructions

Preheat oven to 350°F.

Arrange nuts in single layer on metal baking sheet.

Bake 10 minutes.

Nuts are done when hot and fragrant.

Wrap the hazelnuts in a clean kitchen towel.

Gently rub together until skins are removed.

Serve as garnish to chocolate mousse (recipe above).

President Ford's Plum Torte Chantilly

Plum Torte

Ingredients (6 servings)

½ cup unsalted butter

1 cup sugar

1 cup sifted flour

1 teaspoon baking powder

salt

2 eggs

12 Italian plums, halved & pitted

lemon juice

1 teaspoon cinnamon

Instructions

Preheat oven to 350°F.

Cut plums in half and remove stones.

Beat butter and sugar in a mixing bowl.

Beat in flour, baking powder, eggs and a pinch of salt.

Beat until thoroughly mixed.

Butter a 9 inch springform pan.

Spoon batter into pan.

Arrange plum halves skin side up on top of batter.

Sprinkle lightly with sugar and lemon juice to taste.

Sprinkle with cinnamon.

Bake 1 hour.

Top with Chantilly cream (Recipe follows).

Chantilly cream

Ingredients (6 servings)

2 cups heavy cream

2 tablespoons granulated sugar

1 teaspoon vanilla extract

½ tablespoon finely grated lemon zest

Instructions

Beat cream, sugar, vanilla and zest in a large mixing bowl.

Beat to soft peaks on high speed,

Serve as topping to plum torte (Recipe above).

CHAPTER FIVE

Chef's Dinner

On Celebrity's 965-foot Summit carrying 2034 passengers and 941 crew members, the trans-canal cruise is one of a kind. Sailing through the Panama Canal, the superhuman engineering feat that joins two oceans, and watching as the ship slowly eases through the Panama Canal's locks, with inches to spare on each side, is the experience of a lifetime.

One adventurous port of call on this cruise is the marvelously diverse and unique Belize. It contains the longest barrier reef in the Western Hemisphere, with breathtakingly beautiful beaches and keys. Belize also boasts a 4,000 year history beginning with Mayan rule, until Europeans took over in the 1500s. Belize is widely diverse, with Spanish, Scottish, and British cultures blending. You can take a tour of one of the unspoiled rain forests which house different herbs, as well as wildlife such as jaguars, mountain cows, and howler monkeys in their natural habitat, and thousands of bird species.

Tonight is formal night in the two-level Cosmopolitan Restaurant on the Entertainment Deck at the back of the ship and the Chef's Dinner is served. After a bowl of Chilled Berry and Cumin Yogurt or Petite Marmite Henry IV soup and Crunchy Mixed Green salad, the choice of entrees include Broiled Lobster Tail with a frothy Tarragon and Shallot Butter, or Bucatini with Duck Confit served over pasta with sautéed mushrooms and diced zucchini enhanced with a delicate sauce. Foods are designed to complement each other; a 5-course meal of shrimp cocktail, cream of asparagus soup, caesar salad, veal cordon bleu stuffed with country smoked ham and emmenthal cheese, fried until golden brown, and a blazingly spectacular Baked Alaska. As day 5 of our fantasy cruise ends our reader wonders if they'll ever fit in that tuxedo or evening gown again?

The Chef Presents

We take pride in presenting our Chef's

recommendation

for this evening's meal, foods especially designed
to complement each other and provide a fine
dining experience.

SHRIMP COCKTAIL
Served with Gulf Sauce flavored with Cognac
or a zesty Cocktail Sauce

CREAM OF ASPARAGUS SOUP
An elegant Soup presented in the French Style

CAESAR SALAD
A culinary classic; crisp Romaine Lettuce tossed with
Croutons,
freshly grated Parmesan Cheese and distinctive
Caesar Dressing

VEAL CORDON BLEU
A traditional Dish made with Veal stuffed with
Layers of Country Ham
and Emmenthal Cheese coated with White Bread
Crumbs and served Golden Brown

BAKED ALASKA
A blazingly spectacular Dessert
with layers of Sponge Cake, Ice Cream and Meringue

The Wine Steward
Suggests

The following Wines are recommended to complement the Chef's Selection

Chablis, Joseph Drouhin, Burgundy, France
Cabernet Sauvignon, Jordan, Sonoma, Estate Bottled

WINES BY THE GLASS

White: Meursault, Louis Jadot, Burgundy, France
Red: Cabernet Sauvignon, Reserva, Santa Carolina, Chile

Appetizers

Selected Fruit with a Rum and Coconut Sauce
Shrimp Cocktail   Supreme of Chicken Terrine
Warm Montrachet Cheese and Potato Gratin

Soups

Cream of Asparagus   Petite Marmite "Henry IV"
Chilled Berry and Cumin Yogurt

Salads

Caesar
Tossed Romaine Lettuce, Parmesan Cheese and

Croutons

Panache of Crunchy Mixed Greens
Tarragon   Red Wine Vinaigrette   Caesar
Spicy Tomato

Entrees

Darne of Salmon

Pan Seared, then placed on a bed of Chunky Fruit,
Lychee and Fennel Chutney, Steamed Potatoes

Broiled Lobster Tail

Lobster served with a frothy Tarragon and Shallot
Butter

Bucatini with Duck Confit

Duck Leg cooked in an old traditional style served
boneless over Pasta
with sautéed Mushrooms and diced Zucchini
enhanced with a delicate Sauce

Veal Cordon Bleu

Tender Veal stuffed with Country Smoked Ham and
Emmenthal Cheese,
lightly coated with White Bread Crumbs, shallow
fried until golden brown

Prime Rib of Beef

The finest cut of Roast Beef presented with
Baked Potato, Natural Juice and creamed
Horseradish

Desserts

Baked Alaska   Irish Coffee Torte with a Spirited
Whisky Sauce
Caramelized Pear Napoleon   Bittersweet
Chocolate Cake
No Sugar Added Almond Pear with a Golden Cage
An array of Petit Fours, with the Chef's
compliments
Coffee, Vanilla, Piña Colada or No Sugar Added
Ice Cream
Today's Sherbet with Port Wine Melon Balls

A selection of refined Domestic and Imported
Cheeses
Served with Crackers and Biscuits

The Chef Presents Recipes

Selected Fruit with a Rum and Coconut Sauce

Ingredients (6 servings)

2 mangoes (peeled and cubed)

2 bananas (peeled and sliced)

1 cup fresh pineapple (peeled and cubed)

2 oranges (peeled and segmented)

1 kiwi fruit (peeled and sliced)

¼ cup dark rum

½ cup coconut flakes

Instructions

Set aside coconut flakes.

Mix all the other fruit together in a large glass bowl.

Pour rum over the fruit and mix well.

Refrigerate until chilled.

Toast coconut flakes 2 minutes in a medium sauté pan on high heat.

Coconut is done when toasted golden.

Transfer chilled fruit to tall cocktail glasses.

Sprinkle toasted coconut over the fruit cocktails and serve.

Shrimp Cocktail

Ingredients (6 servings)

3 pints water

½ small onion, sliced

½ small lemon, sliced

2 sprigs fresh parsley

1 teaspoon salt

2 whole peppercorns

¼ teaspoon dried thyme

1 bay leaf

1½ pounds jumbo shrimp, peeled and deveined

½ cup chili sauce

1 tablespoon lemon juice

1 tablespoon prepared horseradish

2 teaspoons Worcestershire sauce

½ teaspoon salt

1 dash cayenne pepper

Instructions

Bring water, onion, lemon, parsley, salt, peppercorns, thyme and bay leaf to a boil in Dutch oven. Mix in shrimp and lower heat to a simmer.

Cook 5 minutes.

Shrimp are done when pink.

Drain and rinse with cold water.

Chill in refrigerate 2 hours.

Combine chili, lemon juice, horseradish, Worcestershire sauce, salt and pepper in a small bowl.

Refrigerate until chilled.

Arrange shrimp on a serving platter with sauce for dipping.

Supreme of Chicken Terrine

Ingredients (6 servings)

2 eggs

1½ pounds boneless chicken breasts

2 cups grated Parmesan cheese

6 slices prosciutto

1 tablespoon minced garlic

8 ounces sliced mushrooms

4 tablespoons butter

1 teaspoon chopped parsley

assorted crackers

salt

fresh ground black pepper

Instructions

Preheat oven to 350°F.

Lightly beat eggs in small bowl.

Season to taste with salt and pepper.

Dip chicken breast into egg mixture,

Roll breast in Parmesan cheese and set aside.

Repeat until all breasts are prepared.

Sauté onions, garlic, and mushrooms in butter 3 minutes until tender.

Season to taste with salt and pepper.

Line a large loaf pan with parchment paper.

Cover bottom of pan with a layer of chicken breasts.

Place a layer of prosciutto over chicken.

Top with sautéed mushrooms and onions.

Repeat the layers.

Sprinkle with parsley.

Cover with parchment paper.

Place a heavy weight on top of the terrine to compress while baking.

Place weighted loaf pan inside a larger pan.

Add water around loaf pan to make a water bath.

Bake 1 hour 20 minutes.

Remove from oven and cool terrine at room temperature.

Refrigerate overnight in pan.

Turn terrine out pan onto a serving platter,

Cut into ¾" slices.

Serve chilled with cracker assortment.

Warm Montrachet Cheese and Potato Gratin

Ingredients (6 servings)

1 cup milk

1 cup whipping cream

1 cup crumbled Montrachet cheese

1 garlic clove, minced

1½ teaspoons salt

¾ teaspoon fresh ground black pepper

1/8 teaspoon ground nutmeg

2 pounds Yukon Gold potatoes

Instructions

Preheat oven to 400°F

Peel potatoes and cut into thin slices.

Butter a small glass baking dish well.

Whisk milk, cream, cheese, garlic, salt, pepper and nutmeg in medium bowl until well combined.

Layer 1/3 of potatoes on bottom of baking dish.

Pour 1/3 of cheese mixture on top of potatoes.

Repeat layering process until you have 3 layers of each.

Bake uncovered 1 hour 15 minutes.

Potatoes are done when tender and top is golden brown.

Serve hot.

Cream of Asparagus

Ingredients (6 servings)

4 cups fresh asparagus

2 cups water

¼ cup green onion, finely chopped

5 tablespoons butter

5 tablespoons all-purpose flour

½ teaspoon salt

¼ teaspoon white pepper

4 cups milk

1 tablespoon vegetable bouillon

Instructions

Trim asparagus and cut into ½" pieces

Place in a large saucepan with 1 cup water.

Bring to a boil.

Cook covered 5 minutes.

Asparagus is done when tender.

Drain and reserve cooking water.

Melt butter in saucepan.

Add onions and Sauté until tender.

Stir in flour, salt and pepper.

Stir until fully combined.

Slowly add and milk, bouillon, reserved cooking water and 1 cup water.

Bring to a boil.

Cook 2 minutes stirring constantly.

When thick and bubbly, add asparagus.

Stir until thoroughly heated.

Serve hot.

Petite Marmite "Henry IV"

Ingredients (6 servings)

¾ pound beef, shoulder palette

1¼ pounds chicken breast

4 ounces bone marrow, sliced

2 quarts water

1 cup dry red wine

1 ounce leeks

1 ounce carrots

¾ ounce celery root

¾ ounce white cabbage

2 teaspoons fresh parsley, chopped

2 teaspoons chervil

1 bay leaf

2 cloves garlic, crushed

6 whole black peppercorns

½ teaspoon nutmeg

salt

fresh ground black pepper

Instructions

Blanch meats 5 to 10 minutes in boiling water.

Put beef in stock pot.

Cover with water.

Simmer 1 hour.

Add chicken, peppercorns, bay leaf, garlic and salt.

Simmer 40 minutes.

Cut vegetables into long thin strips (Julienne).

Add vegetables to stock pot and simmer 20 minutes.

Remove meats from pot.

Cut meats into long thin strips (Julienne).

Return meats to stockpot.

Bring soup to boil.

Add 1 cup dry red wine, bone marrow, parsley, nutmeg and chervil.

Season to taste with salt and pepper.

Chilled Berry and Cumin Yogurt

Ingredients (6 servings)

1½ cups fresh strawberries, sliced

¾ cup fresh raspberries

¾ cup fresh blackberries

1½ cups unsweetened apple juice

1½ cups water

6 tablespoons sugar

3 tablespoons lemon juice

½ teaspoon ground nutmeg

16 ounces black raspberry yogurt

2 teaspoons ground cumin

Instructions

Combine berries, apple juice, water, lemon juice ,nutmeg and sugar in a saucepan,,

Cook 20 minutes on low heat.

Berries are done when softened.

Strain berries and set aside juice.

Press berries through a fine mesh sieve. Discard seeds.

Add berry pulp to reserved juice.

Cover and refrigerate until chilled.

Process chilled berry mix in a blender.

Add in yogurt and cumin.

Cover and blend smooth.

Serve in chilled bowls.

Caesar with Tossed Romaine Lettuce, Parmesan Cheese and Croutons

Ingredients (6 servings)

¼ cup capers, drained and dried

1 teaspoon extra virgin olive oil

3 small garlic cloves, minced

3 anchovy fillets

2 hard-boiled eggs, chopped

¼ cup fresh lemon juice

¼ teaspoon Worcestershire sauce

salt

fresh ground black pepper

½ cup olive oil

½ cup grated Parmesan cheese

Hearts from 2 heads romaine lettuce, leaves roughly torn

6 thick slices sourdough bread, cubed.

Instructions

Preheat oven to 400°F.

In a small bowl, toss capers with 1 teaspoon oil.

Line a baking tray with parchment paper.

Arrange bread cubes on half the tray.

Sprinkle capers in a single layer on the other half.

Drizzle bread with olive oil.

Bake 15 minutes.

Remove from oven when bread is golden and capers are crisped.

Set aside to cool.

Puree garlic, anchovies, lemon juice, Worcestershire sauce and half the Parmesan cheese in a blender.

Slowly add olive oil and continue blending until thoroughly mixed.

Season to taste with salt and freshly ground black pepper.

In a large bowl toss lettuce and eggs until combined.

Drizzle with dressing and toss until well coated.

Divide salad between 6 serving bowls.

Top each salad with croutons.

Sprinkle crispy capers, and remaining Parmesan cheese on salads.

Serve.

Panache of Crunchy Mixed Greens and Red Wine Vinaigrette Dressing

Ingredients (6 servings)

2 tablespoons red wine vinegar

1 tablespoon shallots, chopped fine

1½ teaspoons Dijon mustard

2 tablespoons extra-virgin olive oil

salt

fresh ground black pepper

½ pound mixed greens

1 cup fresh peaches, diced

½ avocado, diced

4 strips crisp cooked bacon, crumbled

1/3 cup feta cheese

Instructions

Combine vinegar and shallots in a small bowl.

Let stand 5 minutes.

Whisk in mustard.

Slowly add oil, whisking constantly until thoroughly combined.

Combine mixed greens, peaches, avocado, bacon and feta cheese in large salad bowl.

Drizzle vinaigrette into the bowl.

Season to taste with salt and pepper.

Toss salad gently until thoroughly coated.

Serve immediately in chilled salad bowls.

Darne of Salmon Pan Pan Seared on a bed of Chunky Fruit, Lychee and Fennel Chutney, Steamed Potatoes

Darne of Salmon Pan Seared

Ingredients (6 servings)

6 center-cut salmon fillets (6 oz. each)

¼ cup fresh lemon juice

¼ cup extra virgin olive oil

salt

fresh ground black pepper

Instructions

Darne is the middle cut of a large fish.

Place salmon darnes in a shallow bowl.

Add lemon juice and olive oil

Season to taste with salt and pepper.

Toss until salmon is thoroughly coated.

Let stand 15 minutes.

Place salmon skin side down in a skillet.

Sear salmon 3 minutes on medium-high heat.

Shake pan and carefully loosen salmon with a spatula.

Lower heat to medium.

Cover skillet and cook 4 minutes.

Salmon darnes are done when skin is crisp and flesh medium

rare.

Serve on bed of chunky fruit (recipe follows).

Bed of Chunky Fruit

Ingredients (6 servings)

6 tablespoons fresh squeezed orange juice

fresh squeezed juice of 2 small limes

fresh grated zest of 1 lime

2½ teaspoons dried mint

3 tablespoons cilantro, chopped

1 large jalapeno pepper, seeded and minced

1½ tablespoons fresh ginger, minced

1 large papaya, seeded and cubed

2 bananas, sliced

3 kiwi fruit, peeled and chopped

1½ pints strawberries, quartered

Instructions

Mix orange juice, lime juice, zest, mint, cilantro, jalapeno
and ginger together in a large bowl. Add fruit.

Toss well and refrigerate overnight.

To serve, divide fruit salad between 6 plates.

Top each fruit bed with a Darne of Salmon (recipe above).

Lychee and Fennel Chutney

Ingredients

10 lychees

4 tablespoons fennel seeds

3 tablespoons fenugreek seeds

2 tablespoons red chili powder

2 teaspoons turmeric powder

3 tablespoons mustard seeds

1½ cups mustard oil

salt

Instructions

Clean lychees and chop into ¾" cubes.

Rub with turmeric powder and salt.

Let stand 30 minutes.

Drain excess moisture.

Grind fenugreek, fennel and mustard seeds to a coarse powder.

Heat mustard oil to smoking point.

Remove from heat and let stand.

Mix ground seeds with red chili powder.

Add half of the mustard oil to the powder mixture.

Rub spice and oil mixture to lychee cubes until thoroughly mixed.

Place lychees in earthenware jar.

Pour in other half of mustard oil.

Add salt to taste and stir well.

Cover jar with muslin cloth.

Let stand 6 days in sunlight, stirring twice daily.

Continue to stir contents of jar twice daily for two weeks.

Serve as relish with Darne of Salmon (recipe above).

Steamed Potatoes

Ingredients (6 servings)

1½ pounds new potatoes

2 tablespoons green onions, diced fine

1 garlic clove, minced

2 tablespoons fresh parsley, chopped

3 tablespoons extra-virgin olive oil

salt

fresh ground black pepper

Instructions

Pour an inch of water in steamer.

Heat on medium-high heat.

Wash potatoes and place in the steamer basket.

Sprinkle with a little sea salt.

When water simmers, place steamer basket on pot and cover.

Cook 20 minutes.

Potatoes are done when tender.

While steaming potatoes, heat olive oil and minced garlic in small skillet on low heat.

Set aside when fragrant.

Remove potatoes from steaming basket.

Place in large bowl.

Add oil and garlic mixture, green onions and parsley.

Season to taste with salt and pepper.

Toss potatoes until well coated.

Serve hot.

Broiled Lobster Tail served with a frothy Tarragon and Shallot Butter

Broiled Lobster Tail

Ingredients (6 Servings)

6 lobster tails

12 tablespoons butter, cut into small pieces

paprika

Instructions

Place a lobster tail on a cutting board belly side down.

With a sharp knife, cut through the back of the lobster tail almost to the end.

Separate the lobster meat from the shell. Keep the tail flesh as intact as possible.

The meat should remain attached to the end of the tail.

Arrange nicely on top of the shell.

Repeat until all lobsters are prepared.

Melt butter and drizzle over lobster meat.

Sprinkle with paprika to taste.

Preheat broiler.

Place lobster on rack 4 inches from heat.

Broil 8 minutes.

When done, lobster meat is white.

Remove from broiler and place the lobster tails on serving plates.

Serve with melted Tarragon Shallot butter (recipe follows).

Tarragon Shallot Butter

Ingredients (6 Servings)

½ cup unsalted butter

3 shallots, minced

2 teaspoons dried tarragon

salt

fresh ground black pepper

Instructions

Combine all ingredients in small bowl.

Mix well.

Melt and serve with broiled lobster Tails (recipe above).

Bucatini with Duck Confit served boneless over Pasta with sautéed Mushrooms and diced Zucchini enhanced with a delicate Sauce

Bucatini with Duck Confit

Ingredients (6 Servings)

¾ pound fresh bucatini pasta

salt

11 ounces duck meat from confit (recipe follows).

1½ ounces butter

3 ounces onion

5 ounces red wine

3 ounces ripe tomatoes, chopped

thyme to taste

marjoram to taste

1 bay leaf

salt

fresh ground black pepper

grated Parmigiano Reggiano cheese

parsley

Instructions

Boil a large pot of salted water.

Add pasta and cook to al dente while preparing sauce.

Melt butter in large skillet.

Sauté onions until browned.

Add duck meat and mix well.

Add wine.

Cook on high heat until liquid reduces in half.

Add herbs, bay leaf and tomatoes.

Season to taste with salt and pepper.

Cook 15 minutes on medium-high heat, stirring occasionally.

When mixture is saucy, taste and adjust seasoning.

While still al dente, drain pasta.

Transfer to sauce skillet and toss well.

Add parsley.

Remove from heat and sprinkle with grated cheese.

Garnish with parsley and arrange on serving dishes.

Serve with sautéed Mushrooms and diced Zucchini (recipe follows).

Duck Confit

Ingredients (6 Servings)

3 tablespoons salt

4 garlic cloves, smashed

1 shallot, peeled and sliced

6 sprigs thyme

fresh ground black pepper

4 duck legs, with thighs

4 duck wings, trimmed

4 cups duck fat

Instructions

Sprinkle 1 tablespoon salt on bottom of large dish.

Sprinkle half the shallots, half the thyme and half the garlic in dish.

Arrange duck pieces in single layer in dish, skin-side up.

Sprinkle remaining salt, garlic, shallots, thyme.

Season to taste with pepper.

Seal and refrigerate 2 days.

Preheat oven to 225°F.

Melt duck fat in small saucepan.

Remove duck pieces from refrigerator.

Brush off salt and seasonings.

Place duck pieces in one tight layer in baking dish.

Pour melted duck fat over pieces.

Duck should be completely covered by fat.

Place baking dish in oven.

Cook 3 hours. Confit will simmer very slowly.

Confit is done when duck is tender and easily pulled from bone.

Remove confit from oven.

Let duck cool to room temperature in the fat.

Refrigerate at least 24 hours. Confit will keep in the refrigerator up to 4 weeks.

Before serving, lift duck pieces from fat.

Remove and discard skin.

Pull duck meat from bone and add to Bucatini (recipe above).

Sautéed Mushrooms and diced Zucchini

Ingredients (6 Servings)

1½ pounds mushrooms

3 small zucchini

Extra virgin olive oil

1½ ounces butter

1 cup dry red wine

3 garlic cloves

Instructions

Clean and halve mushrooms.

Dice zucchini into small cubes.

Place mushrooms and zucchini in large skillet.

Drizzle with olive oil.

Add butter.

Stir well.

Add garlic.

Cover skillet and sauté.

When mushrooms are cooking well, pour in red wine.

Cook until wine evaporates.

Mushrooms are done when garlic caramelizes.

Veal Cordon Bleu stuffed with Country Smoked Ham and Emmenthal Cheese, lightly coated with White Bread Crumbs, shallow fried until golden brown

Ingredients (6 servings)

12 - 2½ ounce veal cutlets, 1/8" thick

12 ounces Emmenthal cheese

6 slices smoked ham, 1/8-inch-thick

1½ cups white bread crumbs

3 teaspoons salt

1¼ teaspoons fresh ground black pepper

1¼ cups all-purpose flour

3 large eggs

3 tablespoons unsalted butter

3 tablespoons extra virgin olive oil

1 lemon cut into 6 wedges

6 sprigs fresh parsley

Instructions

If cutlets are too thick, pound them down to 1/8".

Place between two sheets of plastic wrap and use flat side of meat pounder until 1/8" thick.

Shave cheese thin enough for a double layer for 6 cutlets.

Pat 2 equal cutlets dry on a clean work surface.

Place 1 slice of ham on cutlet.

Trim ham to ¼" smaller than veal.

Place 2 layers of cheese on ham.

Top with second cutlet.

Lightly pound the ¼" border at cutlet edges until sealed.

Repeat for 5 more veal sandwiches.

Line baking sheet with wax paper.

Mix bread crumbs, 1½ teaspoons salt, and ½ teaspoon pepper in baking dish.

Stir together flour, 1 teaspoon salt, and ½ teaspoon pepper in second baking dish.

Whisk eggs with remaining salt and pepper in third baking dish.

Dredge 1 veal sandwich in flour. Brush off excess flour.

Dip in egg to coat,

When excess egg drips off, dredge in bread crumbs and pat until coating sticks.

Place coated veal on a rack set on a baking sheet.

Repeat dredge and coating for remaining veal sandwiches.

Chill1 hour, uncovered.

Let stand 30 minutes at room temperature prior to cooking.

Heat 1 tablespoon butter and 1 tablespoon olive oil in heavy skillet on medium-high heat.

When foaming stops, add 2 veal sandwiches.

Lower heat to medium.

Cook, 4 minutes, turning once.

Cutlet is done when golden both sides.

Transfer veal to serving plates.

Wipe skillet clean.

Repeat process twice to cook 4 more veal sandwiches in remaining butter and olive oil.

Prime Rib of Beef – the finest cut of Roast Beef presented with Baked Potato, Natural Juice and Creamed Horseradish

Prime Rib of Beef au Jus

Ingredients (6 Servings)

5½ lb bone-in prime rib

6 cloves garlic, cut into thin slivers

salt

fresh ground black pepper

2 cups dry red wine

4 cups beef stock

1 tablespoon fresh thyme, chopped

2 teaspoons fresh rosemary, chopped

Instructions

Preheat oven to 450°F.

Cut shallow slits all over prime rib with tip of sharp knife.

Fill each slit with a sliver of garlic.

Season generously salt and pepper.

Place roast, bones down on roasting rack set inside roasting pan.

Insert meat thermometer in centre of roast. Avoid fat or bone.

Oven sear 10 minutes in 450°F oven.

Reduce heat to 350°F.

Roast 2 hours until thermometer reads 140°F for medium-rare. (Roast 2½ hours until thermometer reads 155°F for medium).

Remove roast from oven and transfer to cutting board.

Cover with foil to keep warm.

Place roasting pan of drippings over 2 burners on high heat.

Add wine.

Cook to a reduction on high heat, stirring pan bottom with wooden spoon.

Add beef stock.

Cook until au ju reduces in half.

Whisk in thyme and rosemary.

Season to taste with salt and pepper.

Carve roast into thin slices.

Serve beef with au jus sauce and creamed horseradish (recipe follows).

Creamed Horseradish

Ingredients (6 Servings)

2 cups crème fraîche

½ cup fresh horseradish, peeled and grated

1 tablespoon Champagne vinegar

1 tablespoon chives, minced

1 tablespoon scallions, minced

1 teaspoon salt

1 teaspoon fresh ground black pepper

¼ teaspoon red chile powder

Instructions

Mix all ingredients well in a bowl.

Serve with Prime Rib of Beef au Jus (recipe above).

Baked Potato

Ingredients (6 Servings)

6 – 5 ounce Russet potatoes

extra virgin olive oil

sea salt

Instructions

Set oven rack to middle position.

Preheat oven to 350°F.

Wash potatoes well in cold running water with stiff brush.

Dry potatoes thoroughly with clean towel.

Pierce potatoes deeply with a standard fork at 1" intervals both sides so steam can escape during cooking.

Coat the outside of the potatoes with olive oil.

Sprinkle sea salt on small plate.

Roll potatoes lightly in sea salt.

Place potatoes directly on rack.

Place baking sheet below to catch drippings.

Bake 40 minutes.

Turn potatoes over to prevent browning where in contact with oven rack.

Bake 35 minutes more.

Potatoes are done when skin feels crisp but underlying potato is soft.

Remove potatoes from the oven.

Slit tops lengthways with sharp knife.

Squeeze each end of the potatoes towards the middle.

After potato pop open, loosen fluffy white interior from skin.

Watch out for steam.

Top with butter and serve with Prime Rib of Beef au Jus (recipe above).

Baked Alaska

Ingredients (Serves 6)

1 quart ice cream

3 large eggs

1 cup water

1/3 cup sugar

½ cup flour

½ teaspoon almond extract

1/8 teaspoon cream of tartar

1/8 teaspoon salt

2 teaspoons cornstarch

4 egg whites

¾ cup powdered sugar

2 ounces Cognac

Instructions

Soften ice cream at room temperature for 1 hour.

Bring water to a simmer over low heat in a small sauce pan.

Preheat oven to 425 degrees.

Beat eggs and sugar and almond extract in a small steel mixing bowl over simmering water (double boiler), until the temperature reaches 110-120 degrees.

Remove from heat and continue beating until light and creamy and cooled.

Add flour and cornstarch.

Fold gently. Do not over mix.

Place a sheet of wax paper on a greased baking pan.

Spread the sponge base mixture thinly over the wax paper forming a rectangle.

Bake in oven for 5 minutes.

Remove from oven and let cool.

Remove cake from wax paper.

Cover the bottom and sides of your choice of mold with pieces of cake.

Put the softened ice cream on top of the cake to fill the mold.

Cover the top with more cake.

Freeze for 3 hours.

Beat egg whites, cream of tartar, salt and powdered sugar to a stiff meringue.

Place meringue in a piping bag.

Preheat oven to 425 degrees.

Remove frozen ice cream cake from mold and place on baking tray.

Pipe the meringue over top and sides of the cake.

Sculpture meringue as desired.

Bake in the oven for 4 minutes.

Cake is done when meringue edges are browned.

The meringue surface should be baked, while the ice cream inside remains frozen.

Pour Cognac over meringue surface.

Ignite with a long tapered match.

Serve flaming.

Irish Coffee Torte with a Spirited Whiskey Sauce

Ingredients (Serves 6)

½ cup butter

½ cup caster sugar

1 cup all-purpose flour

1 teaspoon baking powder

2 teaspoons concentrated soluble coffee

2 tablespoons hot water

2 eggs

2/3 cup strong coffee

½ cup sugar

4 tablespoons Irish whiskey

2/3 cup whipped fresh cream

1 heaping tablespoon powdered sugar

chopped hazelnuts.

Instructions

Preheat oven to 350°F.

Dissolve soluble coffee in 2 tablespoons hot water.

Butter an 8" ring pan.

Coat liberally with flour.

Cream butter and sugar together in bowl.

Mix in eggs singly.

Sift flour and baking powder.

Fold in 2/3 of flour.

Add 2 tablespoons dissolved coffee.

Fold in rest of flour mix.

Transfer to pre-buttered ring pan.

Bake 40 minutes at 350°F.

Turn out on rack and let cool.

Clean and set aside ring pan.

Heat strong coffee in saucepan.

Add sugar and heat until fully dissolved.

Boil 1 minute and remove syrup from heat.

Beat in whiskey.

Return cool cake to ring pan.

Pour syrup over cake.

Let soak 8 hours.

Beat powdered sugar and whiskey into whipped cream.

Turn cake out on serving plate.

Frost cake with whipped cream.

Sprinkle with hazelnuts.

Caramelized Pear Napoleon

Ingredients (Serves 6)

Caramelized Pears

4½ tablespoons unsalted butter

3 tablespoons sugar

3 tablespoons brown sugar

2¼ pounds Bosc pears

Puff Pastry

1½ pounds puff pastry (see recipe in *Desert – Extras and Helpful Hints*).

Whipped Cream

1½ cups heavy cream

3 tablespoons sugar

2½ teaspoons vanilla extract

Pistachio Topping

¼ cup raw pistachios

½ tablespoon sugar

½ tablespoon salt

Instructions

Core and cut pears into ½" slices.

Melt butter in skillet on medium heat.

Stir in sugars.

Add pear slicess.

Cook 8 minutes.

Pears are done when slightly tender and juices are syrupy.

Set aside.

Lightly flour work surface.

Roll puff pastry into an 18"x18" square.

Cut rolled pastry into 18 equal 3"x6" pieces.

Pierce pastries all over with fork.

Place pastry slices on baking sheets.

Refrigerate pastry until firm.

Preheat oven to 375 °F.

Place a mesh rack or another baking sheet over pastries to keep them flat as they bake.

Bake 15 minutes.

Pastries are done when golden brown.

Set aside on cooling rack.

Mix ½ tablespoon sugar and ½ tablespoon salt in a bowl.

Add and toss pistachios.

Turn out and spread on baking sheet.

Roast 5 minutes in oven.

Nuts are done when sugar melts and coats them.

Set aside to cool.

Whip cream, sugar and vanilla to soft peaks in mixing bowl.

Take one puff pastry and top with pears and whipped cream.

Place a second puff pastry on top and layer with pears and whipped cream.

Make a third tier of pastry, pears and cream to complete the Napoleon.

Repeat process until you have 6 pear Napoleons.

Sprinkle finished pastries with roasted pistachio nuts.

Bittersweet Chocolate Cake

Ingredients (Serves 6)

6 ounces bittersweet chocolate, chopped

½ cup unsalted butter

¾ cup dark brown sugar

½ teaspoon vanilla extract

9 tablespoons all-purpose flour

¼ teaspoon salt

4 large eggs

½ cup heavy cream

1 teaspoon espresso powder

1 tablespoon sugar

½ cup fresh raspberries

2 tablespoons shaved bittersweet chocolate

Instructions

Preheat oven to 375 degrees °F.

Butter a muffin tin liberally.

Melt chocolate and butter in double boiler set on water at low simmer.

Stir smooth.

Remove from heat.

Whisk in brown sugar and vanilla.

Whisk smooth.

Whisk in flour and salt.

When combined, add eggs singly and continue whisking.

Whisk to a batter.

Pour batter into muffin tray cups.

Bake 15 minutes on center rack.

Turn cakes out on cooling rack.

Let cool 5 minutes.

Beat cream, espresso and sugar to stiff peaks in bowl.

Top cakes with cream.

Garnish with shaved chocolate.

Sprinkle raspberries over cakes.

Serve.

No Sugar Added Almond Pear with a Golden Cage

Ingredients (Serves 6)

1 large egg

1/3 cup sour cream

½ teaspoon almond extract

½ teaspoon vanilla extract

1 cup sifted cake flour

¼ cup sliced unblanched almonds, toasted and ground fine

1/3 cup agave

¼ teaspoon baking powder

¼ teaspoon baking soda

¼ teaspoon salt

6 tablespoons butter

2 pears, poached and sliced in eight equal pieces

Instructions

Preheat oven to 350°F.

Butter a 9" round cake pan.

Arrange pears at bottom of pan.

Combine egg, 4 tablespoons of sour cream, almond extract and vanilla extract in bowl.

In mixer, combine flour, almonds, agave, baking powder, baking soda, and salt.

Mix 30 seconds on low speed until blended.

Add in butter and remainder of sour cream.

Continue mixing until dry ingredients become moist.

Increase speed to medium.

Beat 1½ minutes.

Slowly blend in the egg mixture in batches.

Beat 20 seconds after each blending.

Pour batter into cake pan.

Smooth top with spatula.

Bake for 40 minutes.

Cake is done when a probe stuck in the middle emerges with moist crumbs attached.

Place on cooling rack.

let stand 10 minutes.

Release cake from pan.

Serve immediately.

CHAPTER SIX

Wild for Salmon in Alaska

Holland America's Oosterdam set sail on her maiden

voyage in August 2003. Now she glides through Seattle's

Puget Sound, bound for forested isles, icy blue glaciers and

fir forests close enough to reach out from the deck and brush

with your hand. As our reader spends Day 6 exploring rustic

frontier towns like Ketchikan, chefs prepare the evening

meal passengers will enjoy in the Upper and Lower Vista

Dining Rooms. Tonight's menu features local specialties,

such as Dialogue of Alaskan Salmon Tartare with Avocado

for an appetizer, Shrimp Bisque, and Linguini with Bay

Scallops, clams and mussels in a lightly whipped lobster

sauce.

Freshly Baked Bread
Baguette Rolls – Black Forest Rolls
Sour Dough Bread

Wine Recommendations
Chalone Chardonnay
Ferrari Carano Merlot

APPETIZERS

Pineapple with Alaskan Berries
Freshly picked native berries macerated with tangy pomegranate syrup

Dialogue of Alaskan Salmon Tartare with Avocado
Cold-smoked, pickled and chipltle hot-smoked salmon with lime-avocado-tomato salsa

Golden Baked Brie in Phyllo Dough
Served with a cinnamon-spiced apple-cranberry compote

SALADS

Gourmet Garden Greens in Tomato Shell
Selected baby greens with enoki mushrooms and bell pepper confetti, drizzled with honey
mustard dressing

Caesar Salad
Caesar dressing, parmesan cheese and croutons

SOUPS

Shrimp Bisque
A delicate puree of Alaskan bay shrimps, cream and white wine, served with sourdough
croutons

Oxtail en Croute
Flavorful classical soup slow simmered and served in a crisp pastry crust

ENTREES

Linguini with Seafood and Salmon
Regional bay scallops, clams and mussels in a lightly whipped lobster sauce
and topped with a grilled salmon medallion

Sautéed Shrimps "Provencal"
With garlic, tomato concassé, florets of crisp tender broccoli and sticky rice

Master Chef's Favorite Slow Braised Short Ribs
Simmered in a delicate red wine sauce with dried cherries and served with home-style
mashed potatoes and crisp selected vegetables

Oven Roasted Duck Breast
The old-time favorite, oven roasted until crispy and served with a grand marnier sauce,
braised magenta cabbage, pea pods and william potato

Meritage Noisettes of Beef and Pork
On an earthy bed of calvados-spiked forest mushroom ragoût, with sun dried tomato
risotto, fresh herbs and colorful crisp vegetables

Vegetable Strudel
Summer vegetables and Gouda cheese rolled in phyllo dough and baked till crisp and flaky.
Served with a chive and mushroom sauce and golden rissole potatoes

Or choose one of these Salmon Dishes as
"Holland America Line goes Wild for Salmon"

Hazelnut Crusted Salmon with Sorrel Sauce
Fresh baked fillet with a tarragon and hazelnut topping, served with sorrel sauce,
wild rice and sautéed asparagus and cherry tomatoes
Apricot Glazed Salmon
Baked under a gingery apricot soy glaze and served with a saffron rice timbale
and sautéed leek, carrot and broccoli florets

upon request the above entrées can be served with the sauce on the side
baked potato with sour cream, chives and bacon bits upon request

DESSERTS

Grand Marnier Soufflé
Sweetened foamy egg white and flour baked to lofty heights and served with
vanilla rum sauce

The Master Chef "Premiere"
Beneath Chef Rudi's chocolate hat, we have captured the dynamic
and nuanced flavor of bittersweet chocolate in luxurious mousse,
veritable poem in chocolate surrounded by rubies of macerated berries

NO SUGAR ADDED DESSERT

Sherry Trifle
A sugar-free rendition of the popular English classic

ICE CREAM

Vanilla, Cinnamon
Low Fat Frozen Chocolate Yogurt

NO SUGAR ADDED ICE CREAM

Vanilla or strawberry
Strawberry Sorbet

The Master Chef's Sundae
A generous mound of vanilla ice cream topped with tropical fruit,
whipped cream and sprinkled with roasted macadamia nuts

Sliced Fresh Fruit

Assorted Cheese Plate
A spectrum of full-flavored cheeses (brie, blue cheese, edam, gruyere, herb
pepper, cheddar)
 accompanied by dried fruits and nuts, assorted crisp crackers and French bread

Wild for Salmon in Alaska Recipes

Pineapple with Alaskan Berries

Ingredients (6 servings)

1 ripe pineapple.

1 pint blackberries

1 pint blueberries

1/2 cup raspberries

zest of 1 lime

fresh squeezed juice of ½ lime

1½ tablespoons honey

Juice of 6 pomegranates

1 cup sugar

mint leaves for garnish

Instructions

Peel and core pineapple, cut fruit into chunks.

Whisk lime zest, lime juice and honey together in small bowl.

Mix and toss pineapple, blackberries, blueberries and raspberries in large bowl.

Pour honey-lime mixture on top.

Stir until combined.

Cover and refrigerate overnight.

Combine pomegranate juice and sugar in small saucepan.

Bring to a boil.

Reduce to simmer for 20 minutes, stir frequently.

Syrup is done when liquid reduces to 1 cup.

Remove from heat and let cool.

Cover and refrigerate overnight.

Transfer chilled fruit to serving dishes.

Drizzle syrup over fruit.

Garnish with mint leaves.

Dialogue of Alaskan Salmon Tartare with Avocado

Alaskan Salmon Tartare

Ingredients (4 Servings)

14 ounce fresh Alaskan salmon fillet

4 ounces smoked Alaskan salmon sliced thin

1 garlic clove, chopped very fine

3 shallots, chopped very fine

1 tablespoon fresh squeezed lemon juice

½ teaspoon salt

¼ teaspoon fresh ground black pepper

1 pinch cayenne pepper

4 drops Worcestershire sauce

Instructions

Remove skin from salmon.

Cut fillet and smoked salmon slices into ¼" strips.

Combine salmon in bowl with all other ingredients.

Mix until thoroughly combinedl.

Line four 3" ramekins with plastic wrap, let edges project.

Divide tartare mix evenly amongst ramekins.

Press tops lightly until smooth.

Turn ramekins out onto serving plates.

Remove plastic wrap.

Serve with lime-avocado-tomato salsa (recipe follows).

Lime-avocado-tomato salsa

Ingredients (6 Servings)

1 large tomato, diced

¼ cup red onion, diced

½ jalapeno pepper, minced

5 tablespoons fresh squeezed lime juice

¼ teaspoon salt

1/8 teaspoon fresh ground black pepper

1/2 avocado, pitted and diced

¼ cup fresh cilantro, chopped

1 pinch cayenne pepper

Instructions

Combine tomato, onion, minced jalapeno, lime juice, salt and pepper in bowl.

Add avocado, cilantro and cayenne.

Stir until well mixed.

Refrigerate

Serve chilled with Salmon Tartare (recipe above).

Golden Baked Brie in Phyllo Dough

Baked Brie in Phyllo Dough

Ingredients (6 Servings)

1/8 cup water

1/3 cup flour

4 1/3 tablespoons olive oil

1/8 teaspoon salt

3 tablespoons olive oil

1 half-pound Brie cheese

Instructions

Preheat oven to 350°F.

Sift the flour together with the salt.

Form a well in the center of the sifted flour.

Pour in water and 1 1/3 tablespoons olive oil.

Work until the dough is formed.

Dust flour on a table or board.

Knead the dough on a floured work surface.

Dough is ready to be rolled when smooth and non-stick.

Roll dough into a large rectangle.

Lay a damp towel on top.

Let rest 15 minutes.

Flour hands and work the dough out from center until stretched into a 3 foot square.

Cut dough into 3 equal sheets with a sharp knife.

Place a sheet of phyllo dough work surface.

Brush with 1 tablespoon olive oil.

Lay second sheet over first.

Brush with 1 tablespoon olive oil..

Lay third sheet on top.

Place brie in center and roll up in dough.

Fold ends of dough under and place on baking sheet.

Brush with remaining olive oil.

Bake 15 minutes.

When done phyllo is golden-brown.

Transfer to serving platter.

Serve with cinnamon-spiced apple-cranberry compote (recipe follows).

Cinnamon-spiced apple-cranberry compote

Ingredients (6 Servings)

2 ½ cups cranberry juice

6 ounces dried apples

½ cup dried cranberries

½ cup apple juice

½ cup honey

2 cinnamon sticks, halved

Instructions

Mix juice, apples, cranberries, wine, honey and cinnamon sticks in slow cooker.

Cook 4 hours on low heat.

When liquid is absorbed and fruit is tender, remove cinnamon and discard.

Serve compote warm with baked brie in phyllo dough (recipe above).

Gourmet Garden Greens in Tomato Shell

Greens in Tomato Shell

Ingredients (6 Servings)

12 small roma tomatoes

½ cup chiffonade arugula

2 tablespoons almonds, chopped and toasted

Sea salt for seasoning

Instructions

Score 1-inch jagged cuts lengthways around each tomato with a sharp knife.

Lift tops from tomatoes.

Scoop pulp, leave a ¼ -inch-thick shell.

Season shells with sea salt to taste.

Place shells, cut side down, on paper towels to drain.

Let stand 30 minutes.

Fill shells with greens and serve with enoki mushrooms and bell pepper confetti (recipe follows) drizzled with honey mustard dressing (recipe follows).

Enoki mushrooms and bell pepper confetti

Ingredients (6 Servings)

½ pound enoki mushrooms

1 large red bell pepper

1 large yellow bell pepper

Instructions

Dice peppers and mushrooms into ½" cubes

Serve with Greens in Tomato Shell (recipe above).

Honey mustard dressing

Ingredients (6 Servings)

5 tablespoons honey

3 tablespoons Dijon mustard

2 tablespoons rice wine vinegar

Instructions

Mix all ingredients together in bowl.

Whisk until smooth.

Drizzle over salad (recipe above).

Caesar Salad

Ingredients (6 servings)

¼ cup capers, drained and dried

1 teaspoon extra virgin olive oil

3 small garlic cloves, minced

3 anchovy fillets

2 hard-boiled eggs, chopped

¼ cup fresh lemon juice

¼ teaspoon Worcestershire sauce

salt

fresh ground black pepper

½ cup olive oil

½ cup grated Parmesan cheese

Hearts from 2 heads romaine lettuce, leaves roughly torn

6 thick slices sourdough bread, cubed.

Instructions

Preheat oven to 400°F.

In a small bowl, toss capers with 1 teaspoon oil.

Line a baking tray with parchment paper.

Arrange bread cubes on half the tray.

Sprinkle capers in a single layer on the other half.

Drizzle bread with olive oil.

Bake 15 minutes.

Remove from oven when bread is golden and capers are crisped.

Set aside to cool.

Puree garlic, anchovies, lemon juice, Worcestershire sauce and half the Parmesan cheese in a blender.

Slowly add olive oil and continue blending until thoroughly mixed.

Season to taste with salt and freshly ground black pepper.

In a large bowl toss lettuce and eggs until combined.

Drizzle with dressing and toss until well coated.

Divide salad between 6 serving bowls.

Top each salad with croutons.

Sprinkle crispy capers, and remaining Parmesan cheese on salads.

Serve.

Shrimp Bisque with Sourdough Croutons

Shrimp Bisque

Ingredients (4 Servings)

¼ cup butter

8 ounces shrimp, peeled and deveined

1 rib of celery, finely diced

½ onion, minced

1 bay leaf

1/8 teaspoon thyme

¼ cup sherry

½ cup flour

2 teaspoons paprika

2 pinches fresh ground nutmeg

1 pinch of salt

1 cup milk

1½ cups fresh cream

1 teaspoon tomato paste

Instructions

Melt 1 tablespoon butter in skillet.

Sauté shrimp until pink.

Remove and set aside shrimp.

Add 1 tablespoon butter to skillet.

Sauté celery and onion 7 minutes.

When vegetables are soft, add bay leaf, thyme and sherry.

Cook 2 minutes.

Remove bay leaf.

Purée remaining mixture.

Melt remaining butter in saucepan.

Add flour and stir 3 minutes on low heat.

When roux bubbles, stir in reserved purée.

Add milk, paprika, nutmeg and salt.

Cook on low heat.

Stir until slightly thickened.

Reserve 4 shrimp for garnish.

Chop remaining shrimp.

Add shrimp, tomato paste and cream to pan.

Heat thoroughly without boiling.

When piping hot, pour bisque into 4 serving bowls.

Garnish each bowl with a shrimp.

Serve immediately with sourdough croutons (recipe follows).

Sourdough Croutons

Ingredients (4 Servings)

2 ½ tablespoons olive oil

½ teaspoon fresh crushed garlic

4 slices sourdough bread, cubed

½ teaspoon dried rosemary

1/8 teaspoon salt

¼ teaspoon fresh ground black pepper

Instructions

Preheat oven to 325°F.

Heat olive oil in skillet on medium heat.

Add garlic, rosemary, salt and pepper.

Sauté 2 minutes.

add bread cubes.

Stir until bread is well coated in oil and spices.

Cover baking sheet with parchment paper.

Transfer bread cubes to baking sheet.

Bake 15 minutes, stir every 5 minutes.

Croutons are done when golden-brown.

Remove from oven.

Serve immediately with shrimp bisque (recipe above).

Oxtail en Croute

Oxtail Soup

Ingredients (6 servings)

2 pounds oxtails

½ cup plus 2 tablespoons flour

2 tablespoons beef drippings

2 yellow onions, minced

2 quarts water

2 tablespoons tomato paste

2 teaspoons salt

¼ teaspoon fresh ground black pepper

1 bay leaf

½ teaspoon thyme

3 cloves

2 sprigs parsley

2 carrots, diced

1 stalk celery, diced

1/3 cup port wine

Instructions

Cut oxtails into 1" segments. Trim fat.

Dredge oxtail segments in ½ cup flour.

Cook in beef drippings in large pot on high heat.

When browned, set aside oxtails on paper towels to drain.

Reduce heat to medium.

Add onions and sauté 10 minutes.

When onions are golden, sprinkle in remaining 2 tablespoons flour and mix well.

Cook until lightly browned.

Slowly add water and stir in tomato paste, salt, and pepper.

Tie bay leaf, thyme, cloves, and parsley into a cheesecloth sachet. Add to pot.

Return previously set aside oxtails to pot.

Simmer covered 3 hours.

Oxtails are done when meat is fork tender.

Let cool, skim fat and remove herb sachet.

Separate oxtail meat from bones.

Cut meat into bite-size pieces.

Return meat to pot.

Add carrots and celery.

Simmer covered 15 minutes.

When carrots are tender, add port wine.

Strain and pour oxtail soup into pastry topped ramekins (recipe follows).

Crisp Pastry Crust

Ingredients (6 servings)

20 ounces puff pastry (see recipe in Desert – Extras and
Helpful Hints).

6 egg yolks

6 tablespoons water

2 tablespoons light cream

1 pinch of salt

Instructions

Roll puff pastry dough out to ⅛" thickness.

Cut 6 rounds of pastry a little bigger than the cooking
ramekins.

Fill ramekins until ¾ full of oxtail soup (recipe above).

Mix 2 egg yolks and 2 tablespoons water into a wash.

Rub ramekin rims with egg wash.

Cover ramekins with dough rounds. Pull slightly on edges.

Do not let dough touch the soup.

Refrigerate 1 hour.

Remove ramekins from refrigerator 15 minutes before
baking.

Preheat oven to 400°F

Whisk remaining 4 egg yolks, water, light cream and salt
together in a small bowl.

Egg wash is blended when thick enough to apply without drips.

Brush pastry with egg wash.

Bake 20 minutes.

Oxtail en croute is done when pastry is golden-brown.

Serve hot.

Linguini with Seafood and Salmon

Linguini with Seafood in Lobster Sauce

Ingredients (6 servings)

1 pound fresh linguine

1 ounce butter

salt

8 ounces mussel meat

8 ounces clams (cooked, drained and chopped)

1 pound fresh scallops (raw)

1 cup lobster stock

1 cup heavy cream

Instructions

Cook linguine in pot of salted water with butter.

Drain and set aside when al dente

Heat lobster stock until reduced in half.

Add heavy cream and reduce until slightly thickened.

Whip lightly

Add cooked linguini and drained seafood.

Stir gently 10 minutes.

Serve immediately when seafood is done and sauce is creamy.

Top each serving with a grilled salmon medallion (recipe follows).

Grilled Medallions Of Salmon

Ingredients (6 servings)

1 large salmon fillet

extra-virgin olive oil

Instructions

Preheat grill.

Brush salmon liberally with oil.

Grill salmon, brushing with oil as needed.

When salmon is done, cut into medallions.

Garnish linguini with seafood (recipe above) with salmon medallions.

Serve immediately.

Sautéed Shrimps "Provençal"

Sautéed Shrimps with Garlic

Ingredients (6 servings)

¼ cup extra-virgin olive oil

1½ pounds fresh shrimp, peeled and deveined

salt

fresh ground black pepper

2 garlic cloves, chopped fine

2 tablespoons capers, drained

¼ cup fresh squeezed lemon juice

2 tablespoons parsley, chopped fine

Instructions

Season shrimp with salt and pepper to taste.

Heat 2 tablespoons olive oil in large skillet.

When oil shimmers, add seasoned shrimp.

Sauté 2 minutes on high heat.

When lightly brown and turning opaque, add remainder of olive oil, garlic and capers.

Sauté 30 seconds.

Flip shrimp over. Add lemon juice and half the parsley.

Cover and cook 5 minutes on low heat

Shrimp are done when cooked through.

Transfer shrimp to plates.

Spoon the Provençal sauce from skillet over shrimp.

Sprinkle remaining parsley on top.

Serve with tomato concassé (recipe follows), florets of crisp tender broccoli (recipe follows) and sticky rice (recipe follows).

Tomato Concassé

Ingredients (6 servings)

10 large tomatoes

3 tablespoons extra-virgin olive oil

2 medium shallots, chopped

6 cloves garlic, peeled and chopped

3 tablespoons sherry

1 pinch fesh ground white pepper

6 fresh basil leaves, chopped

3 fresh mint leaves, chopped

1 bunch fresh chives, chopped

Instructions

Remove stems and cut an X skin deep in the bottom of each tomato.

Boil a large pot of water.

Fill a large bowl with ice water.

Immerse tomatoes 20 seconds in the boiling water.

Tomatoes are ready when the cut X deepens and skin loosens slightly.

Transfer tomatoes immediately to the ice bath.

Remove skins. Grasp cut edges and gently slide them off.

Cut tomatoes into quarters and remove core and seeds.

Preheat skillet on medium-high heat.

Add oil and shallot.

Sauté until barely golden.

Add garlic, work it around skillet briefly.

Reduce heat to medium.

Add basil, mint, chives, pepper and sherry.

Sauté 10 minutes.

Fold in tomatoes until combined.

Serve with Shrimps "Provençal" (recipe above).

Florets of Broccoli

Ingredients (6 servings)

8 cups broccoli florets, sliced

2 tablespoons extra-virgin olive oil

½ teaspoon salt

fresh ground black pepper

Instructions

Preheat oven to 450°F.

Toss florets in a bowl with oil, salt and pepper until evenly coated.

Arrange florets on baking sheet.

Roast 20 minutes, stir once halfway through.

Broccoli is done when tender-crisp and light brown in places.

Serve hot with Shrimps "Provençal" (recipe above).

Sticky Rice

Ingredients (6 servings)

4½ cups long grain Thai sweet rice (sticky rice)

Instructions

Put rice in large bowl.

Cover with 3 inches of cold water.

Let soak overnight.

Drain the rice and transfer to steamer basket.

Set basket above boiling water in large pot. Do not let rice contact water.

Cover and let steam 25 minutes.

Rice is shiny and tender when done.

Turn rice out into a basket and cover with cloth.

Keep covered until serving with Shrimps "Provençal" (recipe above).

Master Chef's Favorite Slow Braised Short Ribs

Slow Braised Short Ribs

Ingredients (6 servings)

5 pounds beef short ribs, English cut

1 tablespoon fresh thyme, chopped

1 tablespoon fresh rosemary, chopped

1 teaspoon fresh ground black pepper

2 cups red wine

¼ cup dried Bing cherries

3 tablespoons extra-virgin olive oil

2 onions, chopped fine

2 carrots, chopped fine

1 stalk celery, chopped fine

1 cup fresh tomatoes, chopped

1 tablespoon tomato paste

3 cups chicken broth

1 bay leaf

salt

fresh ground black pepper

Instructions

Put ribs, thyme, rosemary, pepper and wine in large bowl.

Marinate 6 hours refrigerated.

Preheat oven to 450°F.

Take ribs from marinade and pat dry. Set marinade aside.

Put ribs dry on rack in roasting pan.

Roast 45 minutes, then remove from oven.

Reduce heat to 325°F.

Place ribs in bowl.

Drain roasting pan and discard fat.

Add wine marinade to pan.

Heat roasting pan on stovetop on medium-low.

Lightly scrape drippings at bottom of pan to release flavor.

As wine marinade starts to boil, remove from heat. Set aside.

Heat oil in large casserole dish on medium-high.

Sauté onions, carrots and celery until onion is transparent.

Add chopped tomatoes and tomato paste.

Simmer 5 minutes until a little reduced.

Stir while adding wine and drippings to pot.

Continue stirring and mix in chicken broth, bay leaf, cherries salt and pepper.

Add the roasted ribs and bring to very low boil.

Cover and bake in oven for 2¼.

Remove from oven and transfer ribs to pre-warmed serving dish.

Ladle away excess fat from pot.

Boil on medium-high flame until sauce reduces and thickens.

Pour sauce on top of ribs and serve immediately with home-style mashed potatoes (recipe follows) and crisp selected vegetables (recipe follows).

Home-Style Mashed Potatoes

Ingredients (6 servings)

2 pounds Yukon gold potatoes,

¾ teaspoon salt

6 tablespoons heavy cream

3 tablespoons butter

2 tablespoons milk

salt

fresh ground black pepper

Instructions

Peel potatoes and cut into quarters length-ways.

Put potatoes in large pot.

Add ¾ teaspoon salt and water until potatoes are fully submerged.

Bring to full boil.

Reduce heat to rolling simmer and cover.

Cook 20 minutes.

Potatoes are done when crumbly.

Melt butter and cream together in saucepan on low heat.

Drain potatoes through colander.

Transfer hot potatoes to large bowl.

Add melted butter and cream.

Mash with potato masher to desired consistency.

Salt and pepper to taste.

Serve piping hot with slow braised short ribs (recipe above).

Crisp Roasted Vegetables

Ingredients (6 servings)

1½ cup cauliflower florets, sliced

3 cups broccoli, florets, sliced

1½ cups carrots, sliced

¾ cup celery, sliced

½ cup red onion, sliced thin

2 tablespoons extra-virgin olive oil

½ teaspoon salt

fresh ground black pepper

Instructions

Preheat oven to 450°F.

Toss vegetables in a bowl with oil, salt and pepper until evenly coated.

Arrange vegetables on baking sheet.

Roast 20 minutes, stir once halfway through.

Vegetables are done when tender-crisp and light brown in places.

Serve hot with slow braised short ribs (recipe above).

Oven Roasted Duck Breast

Oven Roasted Duck Breast with Grand Marnier Sauce

Ingredients (6 servings)

6 skinless duck breasts

4 tablespoons extra-virgin olive oil

¾ teaspoon salt

½ teaspoon fresh ground white pepper

¾ teaspoon fresh ground coriander

1½ tablespoon sugar

1½ cups fresh squeezed orange juice

1½ tablespoons orange zest

½ cup Grand Marnier

1½ cups butter

Instructions

Rub duck breasts with olive oil, salt, pepper, and coriander.

Wrap breasts in plastic wrap. Refrigerate 2 hours.

Place breasts in large skillet on medium heat.

Cook 4 minutes each side until browned.

Transfer duck breasts to platter.

Cover gently with aluminum foil.

Let stand 5 minutes.

Combine orange juice, sugar, orange zest, and ¼ cup Grand Marnier in saucepan.

Bring to a boil on medium-high heat.

Lower heat to medium.

Simmer until reduced to ¼ cup.

Remove from heat and whisk in butter, a few pieces at a time.

When fully blended, whisk in additional ¼ cup Grand Marnier.

Slice duck diagonally into ¼" slices.

Spoon Grand Marnier sauce onto serving plates.

Arrange the duck on top of sauce.

Serve with braised magenta cabbage (recipe follows), pea pods (recipe follows) and william potato (recipe follows).

Braised Magenta Cabbage

Ingredients (6 servings)

2 large heads of red cabbage

1 tablespoon peanut oil

salt

fresh ground black pepper

1 teaspoon caraway seeds

1 cup dry red wine

1/3 cup red wine vinegar

3 tablespoons sugar

Instructions

Trim, quarter and core cabbages.

Separate cabbage leaves.

Cut out ribs and slice leaves into ¼" strips.

Heat oil on medium heat in saucepan.

When oil shimmers, add a little cabbage, salt and pepper.

Stir-fry until cabbage wilts.

Add a little more cabbage, salt and pepper.

Continue stir-fry process until all cabbage wilts.

Add caraway.

Stir-fry 1 minute.

Add wine and vinegar.

Bring to simmer.

Sprinkle sugar over cabbage.

Stir until well mixed.

Lower heat to medium-low.

Cover on slow simmer 45 minutes. Stir intermittently.

Cabbage is done when most of the liquid is gone and it is soft and shiny.

Remove from the heat and let stand 5 minutes.

Serve hot with oven roasted duck (recipe above).

Pea Pods

Ingredients (6 servings)

2 pounds fresh sugar snap peas

½ cup chicken broth

¼ teaspoon salt

¼ teaspoon fresh ground black pepper

Instructions

Mix ingredients in large skillet.

Bring to a boil.

Cover and let simmer 4 minutes.

Pea pods are done when crisp and tender.

Serve hot using slotted spoon with oven roasted duck (recipe above).

William Potato

Ingredients (6 servings)

1 egg

1 cup bread crumbs

3 cups cold mashed Russet potatoes

1 strand angel hair spaghetti

6 dried bay leaves

Instructions

Preheat oven to 375°F.

Beat egg lightly. Set aside in shallow dish.

Sprinkle bread crumbs on plate. Set aside.

Split mashed potatoes into 6 equal mounds.

Take one potato mound and form into a pear shape by hand.

Coat potato pear in egg.

Roll potato pear in bread crumbs.

Place upright on baking sheet.

Repeat process until all mounds of mashed potato are potato pears.

Bake 20 minutes in oven.

William potatoes are done when golden brown.

Remove from oven and transfer to serving platter.

Snap spaghetti strand into 6 equal pieces.

Stick broken spaghetti strands into tops of potato pears to form stems.

Insert bay leaves at top of potato pears to add a leaf to each pear.

Serve hot with oven roasted duck (recipe above).

Meritage Noisettes of Beef and Pork

Noisettes of Beef and Pork

Ingredients (6 servings)

1 pound beef tenderloin

1 pound pork tenderloin

1 tablespoon fresh sage, minced

1 tablespoon fresh oregano, minced

1 tablespoon salt

½ tablespoon fresh ground black pepper

1 tablespoon extra-virgin olive oil

¼ cup onion, minced

1 cup Meritage red wine

1 cup beef broth

1 tablespoon butter

salt

fresh ground black pepper

Instructions

Heat oil on medium heat in saucepan.

When oil shimmers, add onions.

Sauté until onions are tender and translucent.

Add Meritage red wine.

Cook until syrupy and reduced to ¼ cup of liquid.

Add beef broth.

Cook until reduced to ½ cup of liquid.

Add butter and stir well.

Season to taste with salt and pepper.

Set aside and keep warmed.

Preheat oven to 450°F.

Combine sage, oregano, salt and pepper in bowl.

Sprinkle spices evenly onto platter.

Roll tenderloins in spices on platter until evenly coated.

Preheat sauté pan on medium high.

Add olive oil and heat until oil shimmers.

Place tenderloins in the pan and sear 5 minutes each side.

Let loin rest for 5 minutes.

Slice into ½" thick noisettes.

Drizzle Meritage wine sauce over noisettes.

Serve on bed of calvados-spiked forest mushroom ragoût, (recipe follows) with sun dried tomato risotto (recipe follows) and colorful crisp vegetables (recipe follows).

Calvados-Spiked Forest Mushroom Ragoût

Ingredients (6 servings)

3 ounces dried porcini mushrooms

3 cups boiling water

1 ¼ pound mixed fresh forest mushrooms

1 carrot, chopped

1 shallot, chopped

2 ½ teaspoons tomato paste

5 tablespoons extra-virgin olive oil

1 ½ teaspoons all-purpose flour

2 ½ tablespoons Calvados brandy

1 ½ teaspoons mushroom soy sauce

sea salt

fresh ground white pepper

black truffle oil

Instructions

Pour boiling water on dried mushrooms.

Let soak 20 minutes.

Remove softened mushrooms from soaking liquid with slotted spoon. Set aside.

Strain soaking liquid through a fine mesh. Set aside.

Clean and trim fresh forest mushrooms. Set aside stems and trimmings.

Slice mushroom caps and bodies. Set aside.

Heat 1 tablespoon extra-virgin olive oil on medium heat in 2 quart saucepan.

Add reserved mushroom stems and trimmings, carrots and shallots.

Sauté 5 minutes.

Mushrooms are done when lightly browned.

Add tomato paste.

Cook 2 minutes, stirring constantly.

Add reserved soaking liquid.

Simmer 15 minutes.

Strain mushroom stock through a fine mesh. Discard strained solids.

Set stock aside.

Heat 4 tablespoons extra-virgin olive oil on medium heat in large sauté pan.

Add sliced fresh forest mushrooms.

Sauté 7 minutes.

Mushrooms are done when well browned.

Add reserved soaked mushrooms.

Stir 1 minute.

Add flour.

Stir continually 3 minutes.

When flour is lightly browned, add Calvados.

Gently shake sauté pan while tipped to ignite and flame off brandy.

Add 1 cup reserved mushroom stock.

Add soy sauce.

Simmer gently 20 minutes on low heat.

Season to taste with salt and pepper.

Add black truffle oil to taste immediately before serving.

Place a bed of ragout on each serving plate.

Arrange Noisettes of Beef and Pork (recipe above) on top of ragout.

Serve with sun dried tomato risotto (recipe follows) and colorful crisp vegetables (recipe follows).

Sun-Dried Tomato Risotto

Ingredients (6 servings)

4 tablespoons Butter

2 tablespoons extra-virgin olive oil

½ onion, diced

3 garlic cloves, minced

2 cups Arborio Rice

8 sun-dried tomatoes, minced

7 cups low sodium chicken broth

salt

fresh ground black pepper

1 cup Parmesan cheese, grated

¼ cup heavy cream

fresh parsley leaves, chopped fine (for garnish)

Instructions

Heat broth in saucepan. Set aside.

Heat butter and olive oil in dutch oven on medium heat.

Add onions and garlic.

Cook 4 minutes.

Add rice.

Stir well until rice is evenly coated.

Cook 3 minutes, stirring gently.

Stir and cook on medium-low heat until almost all liquid absorbs.

Add minced sundried tomatoes. Stir well.

Add broth, a cup at a time. Stir gently as rice absorbs the liquid.

Repeat until rice is done (8 cups broth).

When done rice will be firm but not crunchy.

Remove from heat.

Stir in Parmesan cheese and heavy cream.

Season to taste with salt and pepper.

Serve hot with noisettes of beef and pork (recipe above).

Colorful Crisp Vegetables

Ingredients (6 servings)

1½ cup cauliflower florets, sliced

3 cups broccoli, florets, sliced

1½ cups carrots, sliced

¾ cup celery, sliced

½ cup red onion, sliced thin

2 tablespoons extra-virgin olive oil

½ teaspoon salt

fresh ground black pepper

Instructions

Preheat oven to 450°F.

Toss vegetables in a bowl with oil, salt and pepper until evenly coated.

Arrange vegetables on baking sheet.

Roast 20 minutes, stir once halfway through.

Vegetables are done when tender-crisp and light brown in places.

Serve hot with noisettes of beef and pork (recipe above).

Vegetable Strudel With Chive and Mushroom Sauce and Golden Rissole Potatoes

Vegetable Strudel

Ingredients (6 servings)

1/8 cup water

1/3 cup flour

1 1/3 tablespoons olive oil

2 Carrots, sliced thin

½ pound green beans

½ pound broccoli florets

6 mushrooms, sliced

1 stalk celery,

¼ pound bean sprouts

1 onion, chopped fine

1½ cups Gouda cheese, grated

1 egg, beaten

Instructions

Preheat oven to 400°F.

Sift the flour together with the salt.

Form a well in the center of the sifted flour.

Pour in water and 1 1/3 tablespoons olive oil.

Work until the dough is formed.

Dust flour on a table or board.

Knead the dough on a floured work surface.

Dough is ready to be rolled when smooth and non-stick.

Roll dough into a large rectangle.

Lay a damp towel on top.

Let rest 15 minutes.

Flour hands and work the dough out from center.

Fold pastry into an oblong, twice.

Roll firmly until thin again.

Combine vegetables, mushrooms and cheese.

Spoon mix onto middle of pastry sheet.

Brush beaten egg on pastry edges.

Roll pastry into a tube around filling.

Crimp to close ends.

Cut 1 inch slits in top of strudel.

Bake 40 minutes.

Strudel is done when golden.

Transfer to serving platter.

Serve hot with chive and mushroom sauce (recipe follows)
and golden rissole potatoes (recipe follows).

Chive and Mushroom Sauce

Ingredients (6 servings)

2 tablespoons extra-virgin olive oil

1 cup fresh mushrooms, sliced

¾ cup chives, minced

2 tablespoons all-purpose flour

¼ cup chicken broth

2 cups heavy cream

1 pinch nutmeg

salt

fresh ground black pepper

Instructions

Sauté mushrooms and chives 2 minutes in oil in large skillet.

Stir in flour.

Whisk in broth slowly until well blended.

Stir in cream, nutmeg, and season to taste with salt and pepper.

Bring to boil.

Stir 3 minutes.

Sauce is ready when thickened.

Serve hot with vegetable strudel (recipe above).

Golden Rissole Potatoes

Ingredients (6 servings)

3 pounds russet potatoes

1½ teaspoons salt

6 tablespoons melted butter

3 tablespoons extra-virgin olive oil

Instructions

Peel and wash potatoes.

Scoop out potato balls with French ball cutter.

Drop balls in cold water.

Soak 15 minutes.

Preheat oven to 350°F.

Drain and place potato balls in saucepan.

Cover with water and add salt.

Boil 5 minutes

Drain and place potato balls, butter and olive oil in baking pan.

Stir until potatoes are evenly coated.

Bake 20 minutes. Turn over halfway.

Potatoes are done when evenly golden brown all over.

Serve hot with vegetable strudel (recipe above).

Grand Marnier Soufflé with Vanilla Rum Sauce

Grand Marnier Soufflé

Ingredients (6 servings)

¾ cup fresh squeezed orange juice

¼ cup fresh squeezed lemon juice

2 cups sugar

¼ cup butter

¼ cup flour

1/8 cup Grand Marnier liqueur

4 egg yolks

6 egg whites

1 pinch salt

grated zest of 1 orange

Instructions

Boil orange juice, lemon juice and sugar in saucepan.

Stir until sugar dissolves.

Keep heated on low heat.

Melt butter on medium heat in saucepan.

Add flour. Whisk smooth.

Whisk 3 minutes as butter bubbles. Do not let butter brown.

Whisk in the reserved hot sugared juices.

Whisk until boiling and thickened.

Remove from heat.

Add Grand Marnier.

Cool until slightly hot.

Whisk in egg yolks, one by one.

Cool to lukewarm.

Whisk in egg whites.

Set aside or refrigerate.

Butter inside of 6 soufflé dishes.

Cut 4" wax paper strips long enough to wrap each dish and overlap 1".

Double strips over lengthwise to form collars.

Butter one side of folded strip along the crease.

Wrap soufflé dish with collar, butter side in.

Attach collar with masking tape.

mix orange zest with 1 cup sugar.

Sprinkle mixture over dish bottom, sides and collar.

Shake until thoroughly coated. Discard excess.

Place egg whites in bowl.

Add salt and beat to stiff peaks.

Gently fold a heaping spoonful of whites into cooled juice, sugar and egg yolk mixture.

Add remaining whites.

Fold in quickly but gently.

Spoon into orange-sugared soufflé dishes.

Heap mixture slightly over tops of dishes.

Sprinkle crown of soufflé with orange zest and sugar mix.

Bake 25 minutes in 325°F water bath.

Remove collars.

Serve with vanilla rum creme anglaise (recipe follows).

Vanilla Rum Creme Anglaise

Ingredients (6 servings)

¾ cup rum

2 teaspoons vanilla extract

6 egg yolks

2/3 cup sugar

1¼ cups heavy cream

Instructions

Heat saucepan on medium heat.

Add rum.

Tilt and gently shake pan while tipped to ignite and flambé rum

Set syrup aside.

Heat double boiler with boiling water on bottom and mixing bowl above but not touching water.

Put egg yolks and sugar in mixing bowl.

Whisk continuously until yolks and sugar are well combined

Add heavy cream. Continue to whisk.

When sauce is a smooth, shiny cream, Add reserved rum syrup.

Mix well and let creme Anglaise cool.

Serve over Grand Marnier soufflé (recipe above).

The Master Chef "Premiere"

Chocolate Mousse

Ingredients (6 servings)

3 ounces bittersweet chocolate, chopped fine.

6 egg yolks

3/8 cup sugar

1 pinch salt

3 tablespoons unsweetened cocoa powder

1¼ cups heavy cream

6 molded bittersweet chocolate hats.

Instructions

Whisk yolks, sugar and salt 3 minutes in double boiler until sugar dissolves.

Remove from heat and whisk in chopped chocolate.

When melted, smooth and thickened let cool to room temperature.

Whip cream to soft peaks in bowl.

Whisk half the whipped cream into chocolate mixture.

Gently fold in other half of whipped cream with spatula.

Divide mousse between six serving dishes.

Refrigerate until well chilled.

Remove mousse from refrigeration and let stand 15 minutes.

Top with chocolate hats.

Surround mouse with macerated berries (recipe follows).

Macerated Berries

Ingredients (6 servings)

2 cups raspberries

1 cup blueberries

1 cup strawberries, halved

2 tablespoons powdered sugar

fresh squeezed juice of 1 lemon

grated zest of 1 lemon

½ cup Grand Marnier

Instructions

Place berries in bowl.

Sprinkle sugar to coat berries.

Pour Grand Marnier over berries.

Add lemon juice.

Add zest.

Mix lightly.

Cover bowl and refrigerate overnight.

Serve with chocolate mousse (recipe above)

No Sugar Added Sherry Trifle

Ingredients (6 servings)

1 sponge cake, cut into cubes

1 cup seedless raspberry jam

6 tablespoons sherry

12 ounces fresh raspberries

2 ounces ratafia biscuits

1 pint milk

1 vanilla pod

4 egg yolks

1 tablespoon honey

1½ tablespoons cornflour

¾ pint heavy cream

2 ounces almonds, sliced and toasted

fresh raspberries for garnish

Instructions

Spread each cake cube thinly with raspberry jam.

Place cubes in the bottom of large glass bowl.

Sprinkle sherry over top of cake cubes.

Layer raspberries over cake.

Crush ratafia biscuits over raspberries.

Refrigerate 4 hours.

Heat milk and vanilla pod in saucepan on medium heat. Do not let boil.

Transfer to pitcher. Let infuse 10 minutes.

Remove vanilla pod.

Whisk egg yolks, cornflour and honey in a bowl until combined.

Whisk in vanilla infused milk.

Strain back to saucepan through fine mesh.

Stir constantly on low heat. Do not let boil.

Cook until the custard is thickened and will coat the back of a tablespoon.

Transfer custard to cooled bowl.

Set aside to cool.

Spoon a layer of cold custard on top of raspberries.

Whip heavy cream to soft peaks in bowl..

Reserve quarter of the whipped cream and spoon remainder on top of the custard.

Smooth surface and carefully spread across full width of bowl.

Whip reserved cream to stiff peaks.

Decorate top of trifle with piped cream.

Garnish top with raspberries.

Refrigerate 2 hours.

Serve chilled.

CHAPTER SEVEN

Debarkation -- Farewell Dinner

Acclaimed Italian architect Renzo Piano designed the all-white Regal Princess to stand out from other cruise ships with its many distinctive features. Unlike other ships, it has a single stack, a dolphin-like prow and a domed observation lounge that curves around the front of the ship for dazzling views.

Our fantasy cruise ends on Day 7 in the "City by the Bay," San Francisco. The Princess sails under the graceful Golden Gate Bridge, one of the most famous and recognizable landmarks in the U.S. Debark and enjoy the old-world charm, hilly streets, famous bridges and historic cable cars.

The bustling Fisherman's Wharf was once home to San Fran's fishing fleet. Today it hosts seafood vendors, souvenir shops and tourist attractions, such as the Wax Museum, vintage sea craft from World War II, and a historic maritime park.

The Landfall Dinner is the Princess's Farewell Dinner, a last hurrah of gourmet treats before heading for home and the gym to work off that pound a day they say you gain on a cruise.

REGAL PRINCESS
LANDFALL DINNER
APPETIZERS

Avocado Boat with Seafood in a Lime-Cilantro
Vinaigrette
Citrus Fruit Collection with Zucchini Bread and
Toasted Almonds
Vol-au-Vent a la Reine
*Creamed Chicken, Sweetbreads and Mushrooms in
a Puff Pastry Case*

SOUPS

Philadelphia Pepper Pot
Fresh Green Asparagus Purée with Tapioca Pearls
and Croutons
Chilled Curried Pumpkin and William Pear Cream
Soup

SALAD

Grilled Vegetables and Hearts of Romaine Lettuce
*Honey Mustard, Champagne Vinaigrette or Low-Fat
Cassis Chive Dressing*

ENTREES
PRINCESS FAVORITE

Linguine alle Vongole
*Long Pasta Noodles and Roasted Sweet Bell
Peppers in a
Light Béchamel of Poached Clams and Chopped
Fresh Parsley*

Freshwater Tilapia in a Parsley-Crumb Coat
*Sautéed Fish Filet in a Tasting Brown Sauce,
Enhanced with*

Pink Pepper Corn, Served over Jasmine Rice and a Variety of Vegetables

Sea Scallops Mediterranean Fashion
Presented on a Bed of Eggplant, Tomatoes, Zucchini, Black Olives, Capers and Fresh Herbs
Young Tom Turkey and All the Trimmings
*Whole-Roasted with Dried Fruit Stuffing, Giblet Gravy,
Cranberry Sauce, Corn Pudding and Glazed Sweet Potatoes*

Prime Rib au Jus
Roast Beef with Natural Gravy, Grilled Tomato, Corn-on-the-Cob and Brioche Potato

AFTER DINNER PLEASURE

FROM THE SHIP'S PASTRY

The Princess Love Boat Dream
Fluffy Dark Swiss Chocolate Mousse, Flavored With Lady Godiva Liqueur

Fresh Fruit Gratin
A Selection of Premium Mixed Fruits With Warm Honey Zabaglione

Brandy Alexander Pie
Old Brandy-Style Bavarian Cream Pie, Decorated with Chocolate Rice Crispies

FROM THE SHIP'S ICE CREAM FOUNTAIN

A Daily Selection of Ice Cream and Sorbet

OUR INTERNATIONAL SELECTION OF CHEESE
Presented with Crackers and Biscuits

Nature's Freshest Seasonal Fruits
Exquisitely Presented in Delightful Medley

Landfall Dinner Recipes

Avocado Boat with Seafood in a Lime-Cilantro Vinaigrette

Ingredients (6 servings)

1½ cups crab, cooked and flaked

1½ cups shrimp (small), cooked

6 tablespoons cucumber, diced

¼ teaspoon paprika

3½ cups cider vinegar

2 tablespoons fresh cilantro, chopped

1 teaspoon lime zest

2 tablespoons lime juice

1 tablespoon honey

salt

fresh ground black pepper

¼ cup olive oil

Instructions

Mix crab, shrimp and cucumber in bowl.

Season to taste with salt and pepper.

Cover and refrigerate until chilled..

Halve each avocado lengthwise and remove the stone.

Scoop out middle of each half. Leave ½" of avocado on the skin.

Spoon the chilled seafood into scooped avocado shells.

Sprinkle tops with paprika.

Whisk vinegar, cilantro, lime zest, lime juice, honey and ¼ teaspoon salt in bowl,

Slowly add in oil while continuing to whisk.

When mixed smooth and well whisked, drizzle over avocado boats.

Serve immediately.

Citrus Fruit Collection with Zucchini Bread and Toasted Almonds

Citrus Fruit Collection

Ingredients (6 servings)

1 cup naval orange segments

1 cup Cara Cara orange segments

1 cup pink grapefruit segments

2 cups fresh cut pineapple cubes

1½ cups strawberries, sliced

1 cup seedless grapes

¼ cup fresh squeezed orange juice

¼ cup squeezed fresh lime juice

3 tablespoons fresh cilantro, chopped fine

2 tablespoons honey

Instructions

Place fruit in large bowl.

Toss until well mixed.

Combine juices, cilantro and honey in bowl.

Stir until well mixed.

Pour over fruit.

Toss gently until fruit is coated with mixture.

Cover and refrigerate 1 hour.

Serve chilled with Zucchini Bread and Toasted Almonds (recipe follows).

Zucchini Bread and Toasted Almonds

Ingredients (6 servings)

1½ cups all-purpose flour

1 teaspoon baking soda

1 teaspoon baking Powder

¼ teaspoon ground cinnamon

1 pinch grated nutmeg

½ cup sugar

2 tablespoons light brown sugar

2 eggs

½ cup vegetable oil

1 teaspoon vanilla essence

¼ teaspoon salt

1½ cups zucchini, shredded

¼ cup raisins

¼ cup almonds, sliced

Instructions

Preheat oven to 350°F.

Line 9"x5" loaf pan with parchment paper.

Brush insides with butter.

Mix flour, baking soda, baking powder, cinnamon and nutmeg together in large bowl.

Whisk well and set aside.

Beat eggs in large bowl until frothy.

Add sugar, oil, vanilla and salt.

Mix well.

Add flour mixture.

Mix batter well.

Fold in zucchini and raisins.

Sprinkle 2 tablespoons of almonds in loaf pan.

Pour in batter.

Sprinkle remaining almonds on top of batter.

Bake 40 minutes on center rack of oven.

Set on cooling rack 10 minutes.

Slice and serve with citrus fruit collection (recipe above)

Vol-au-Vent a la Reine

Ingredients (6 servings)

½ pound puff pastry (see recipe in *Desert – Extras and Helpful Hints*).

1 egg, beaten

1 tablespoon water

3 large chicken breasts

1½ cups veal

3 bay leaves

2 cloves

1 teaspoon peppercorns

2 tablespoons butter

½ cup all-purpose flour

½ cup chicken stock

1 teaspoon sea salt

1 teaspoon nutmeg

1½ cups fresh mushrooms

½ cup white wine

Instructions

Chill ½ pounds of puff pastry.

Line baking sheet with parchment paper.

Lightly flour a clean work surface.

Roll dough into a rectangle 3/8" thick.

Transfer to baking sheet.

Refrigerate 10 minutes.

Use a 3" cutter to cut 12 circles of dough.

Use a 1½" cutter to cut centers from six rounds to form rings for the sides of the vols-au-vent. Set center cuts aside for caps.

Mix beaten egg and water well to create egg wash.

Lightly prick solid rounds with fork. Do not perforate.

Brush lightly with egg wash.

Place dough rings on top of bottom rounds and press lightly, forming sides.

When adhered, brush top rings lightly with egg wash.

Prick and egg wash the caps.

Refrigerate assembled vols-au-vent on lined baking sheet.

Preheat oven to 400°F.

Remove from refrigerator and cover with silicon baking mat.

Bake vols-au-vent 15 minutes until risen and starting to brown.

Lower oven to 350°F.

Remove silicon mat.

Gently press down any risen centers.

Bake 15 minutes uncovered.

Vol-au-vent shells are done when layers are golden brown.

Caps will bake faster than the shells. Remove when done.

Remove shells to cooling rack.

Put chicken, veal, bay leaves, cloves and peppercorns in large pot of cold water.

Bring to slow boil,

Lower heat to medium-low.

Cook 2 hours.

Combine butter and flour.

Sauté into a roux for the sauce.

Thicken sauce with chicken stock to desired consistency.

Season to taste with salt, pepper and nutmeg.

Cut meats into small cubes.

Sauté mushrooms in butter.

Add white wine.

Combine everything into the sauce.

Mix well.

Warm the vol-au-vent shells.

Fill warmed vol-au-vent shells and serve hot.

Philadelphia Pepper Pot

Ingredients (6 servings)

2 pounds honeycomb tripe

1½ pounds veal knuckle

3 carrots, sliced

1 large onion, sliced

½ cup celery, cut

2 tablespoons fresh parsley, chopped

1 teaspoon dried marjoram

1 teaspoon summer savory

1 teaspoon dried basil

1 teaspoon dried thyme

3 teaspoons salt

½ teaspoon black pepper

¼ teaspoon cayenne

4 cloves

2 bay leaves

2 potatoes, cubed ½ inch

Instructions

Place tripe in Dutch oven.

Cover with water.

Add 2 teaspoons salt.

Cover and bring to boil.

Lower heat to a slow simmer

Cook 4 hours.

Drain tripe when clear and jelly like.

Cut tripe into ½" cubes.

Refrigerate.

Place veal knuckle, carrots, onion, celery, parsley and herbs in 4-quart Dutch oven.

Add 6 cups water.

Add 1 teaspoon salt.

Cover and bring to boil.

Lower heat to a slow simmer

Cook 2 hours.

Strain when meat comes off bone.

Discard bones and vegetables.

Refrigerate.

Skim fat from refrigerated broth.

Heat 4 cups veal broth.

Add tripe and potatoes.

Simmer 15 minutes.

When potatoes are tender, serve piping hot.

Fresh Green Asparagus Purée with Tapioca Pearls and Croutons

Asparagus Purée with Tapioca Pearls

Ingredients (6 servings)

1½ pounds green asparagus

1½ tablespoons butter

1 large brown onion, sliced fine

6 garlic cloves, sliced fine

salt

fresh ground white pepper

1 cup water

2 ounces medium pearl tapioca

Instructions

Snap hard ends snapped off asparagus.

Cut 1½" long spears from asparagus tops. Set aside.

Chop stems fine.

Melt butter in small saucepan.

Add onion and 3 garlic cloves.

Season to taste with salt and pepper.

Cook 15 minutes on low heat.

When onion is soft, add asparagus stems and water.

Simmer 15 minutes on low heat.

Asparagus is done when soft.

Blend to a smooth purée.

Set aside and keep warmed.

Rinse tapioca well.

Place pearls in large pot of boiling water.

Cook 15 minutes on high heat, stirring frequently.

Drain when pearls are cooked al dente with a small white center.

Rinse and stir into warm asparagus purée.

Serve hot with croutons (recipe follows).

Croutons

Ingredients

3 tablespoons olive oil

1 large day-old baguette

1 teaspoon salt

Instructions

Cut bread into 1-inch cubes.

Heat 3 tablespoons olive oil in sauté pan on medium heat.

Sauté bread cubes 5 minutes, stirring constantly.

Croutons are done when toasted and golden all around..

Remove and drain croutons on paper towels.

Serve with asparagus purée with tapioca pearls (recipe above).

Chilled Curried Pumpkin and Williams Pear Cream Soup

Ingredients (6 servings)

2 tablespoons butter

1 cup onion, chopped

2 garlic cloves, chopped fine

1½ teaspoons curry powder

¼ teaspoon ground nutmeg

¼ teaspoon allspice

½ teaspoon salt

¼ teaspoon ground white pepper

1 small sugar pumpkin

2 Bartlett pears, cored, peeled, and diced (Williams pear in the UK)

1 tablespoon olive oil

3 cups chicken broth

1 cup half and half

½ cup apple nectar

Instructions

Preheat oven to 375°F.

Line baking sheet with parchment paper.

Toss pears on baking sheet with olive oil, salt, and pepper until coated.

Place in oven and bake 15 minutes. Turn halfway through.

Pears are done when still firm with golden brown edges.

Set aside.

Rinse pumpkin well.

Cut into large pieces.

Line roasting pan with aluminum foil.

Place pumpkin pieces cut side down in roasting pan.

Add a small amount of water to pan.

Roast 1 hour at 375°F.

Pumpkin is done when knife tender.

Let pumpkin pieces cool.

Cut off outer skin.

Purée until smooth.

Melt butter in large saucepan on medium-high heat.

Add onion and garlic.

Sauté 4 minutes. Stir constantly.

Add spices, salt and pepper.

Cook 30 seconds until aromatic.

Stir in pumpkin.

Add broth.

Bring to boil, then lower to low heat.

Cook 15 minutes. Stir frequently.

Stir in cooked pears

Add half and half and apple nectar.

Simmer 3 minutes on low heat until hot.

Serve warm.

Grilled Vegetables and Hearts of Romaine Lettuce

Grilled Vegetables and Hearts of Romaine Lettuce

Ingredients (6 servings)

3 hearts romaine lettuce

3 tablespoons extra-virgin olive oil

2 pints cherry tomatoes

2 yellow onions

2 red bell peppers,

2 yellow bell peppers

2 green bell peppers

½ cup extra-virgin olive oil

salt

fresh ground black pepper

½ cup fresh basil

Instructions

Preheat grill to medium.

Cut romaine hearts in half long ways.

Brush with olive oil. Set aside.

Cut peppers into quarters. Remove ribs and seeds.

Cut onions into ½" rings.

Place tomatoes, onions and peppers in large bowl.

add olive oil.

Toss well until vegetables are coated.

Season to taste with salt and pepper.

Place lettuce and seasoned vegetable on grill.

Grill 6 minutes, turning intermittently.

Lettuce is done when charred and slightly wilted.

Vegetables are done when charred and tender.

Season lettuce to taste with salt and pepper.

Remove everything to serving platter.

Sprinkle with basil.

Serve with choice of dressings (recipes follow).

Honey Mustard Dressing

Ingredients (6 servings)

¼ cup honey

¼ cup white wine vinegar

1 teaspoon Dijon mustard

1 teaspoon poppy seeds

2 tablespoons lemon juice

¼ teaspoon salt

¾ cup extra virgin olive oil

Instructions

Combine all but olive oil in blender.

Slowly stream in olive oil while blending.

Dressing is done when smooth and creamy.

Refrigerate 30 minutes.

Drizzle over grilled vegetables and hearts of romaine lettuce (recipe above).

Champagne Vinaigrette Dressing

Ingredients (6 servings)

1 cup extra virgin olive oil

¼ cup champagne vinegar

½ cup champagne

¾ teaspoon fresh ground white pepper

1 pinch sugar

Instructions

Combine all but olive oil in blender.

Slowly stream in olive oil while blending.

Dressing is done when smooth and creamy.

Drizzle over grilled vegetables and hearts of romaine lettuce (recipe above).

Low-Fat Cassis Chive Dressing

Ingredients (6 servings)

2 tablespoons extra-virgin olive oil

1 tablespoon white-wine vinegar

1 tablespoon crème de cassis

½ teaspoon Dijon mustard

¼ teaspoon sugar

1 tablespoon water

1 tablespoon fresh chives, chopped very fine

¼ teaspoon salt

¾ teaspoon fresh ground black pepper

Instructions

Combine all ingredients in blender.

Process until smooth and creamy.

Drizzle over grilled vegetables and hearts of romaine lettuce (recipe above).

Linguini alle Vongole

Ingredients (6 servings)

6 red bell peppers

1 shallot, chopped

4 garlic cloves, chopped

¼ cup extra-virgin olive oil

½ cup white wine

¼ teaspoon chile flakes

4 tomatoes, chopped

1 pound linguine

4 pounds clams

½ cup parsley, chopped

Instructions

Scrub and rinse clams.

Preheat broiler.

Halve peppers long ways.

Remove seeds and ribs.

Broil skin side up until skins char.

Freeze roasted peppers 10 minutes to loosen skins.

Rub off blackened skins.

Chop skinned peppers and set aside.

Boil a large pot of salted water.

Heat oil in large skillet on medium-high heat.

Add shallot and garlic.

Sauté 3 minutes until soft.

Add wine.

Cook 1 minute.

Stir in chile and tomatoes.

Cook 2 minutes.

Put linguine in boiling water.

Cook 5 minutes.

While linguine cooks add clams to garlic and pepper mix.

Raise to high heat.

Cover skillet and cook 5 minutes.

Drain pasta and add to clam skillet.

Cover and cook 5 minutes more. Stir intermittently.

Dish is done when clams open and pasta is al dente.

Remove and discard unopened clams.

Transfer to large bowl.

Sprinkle with parsley.

Toss pasta and clams with parsley until well mixed.

Serve hot.

Freshwater Tilapia in a Parsley-Crumb Coat

Freshwater Tilapia in a Parsley-Crumb Coat

Ingredients (6 Servings)

6 tilapia fillets.

2 eggs

3 cups bread crumbs.

3 tablespoons fresh parsley, chopped fine

3 tablespoons extra-virgin olive oil

1½ cups all-purpose flour

salt

fresh ground black pepper

Instructions

Season tilapia fillets with salt and pepper to taste.

Let sit 15 minutes.

Whisk eggs in medium bowl

Combine flour, salt and pepper to taste.

Spread in shallow dish.

Combine bread crumbs, chopped parsley, salt and pepper to taste.

Spread in second shallow dish.

Coat fillet both sides with flour mixture.

Dip coated fillet in egg.

Press coated fillet into bread crumbs. Lightly press both sides.

Repeat process until all fillets are coated.

Heat oil in large skillet on low heat.

Place fillets carefully into skillet.

Sauté until golden brown both sides.

Serve hot with brown sauce enhanced with pink peppercorn (recipe below), jasmine rice (recipe below) and a variety of vegetables (recipe below).

Brown Sauce Enhanced With Pink Peppercorn

Ingredients (6 servings)

2 tablespoons soy sauce

1 cup soup stock

¼ cup red wine

2 tablespoons cornstarch

1 pinch MSG

1 tablespoon sugar

½ teaspoon molasses

¼ teaspoon salt

juice of 1 ginger root

1 teaspoon pink peppercorns, ground

Instructions

Heat soup stock on medium high heat.

Stir in soy sauce, MSG, salt, sugar, ginger juice and molasses.

Lower heat and let simmer 10 minutes.

Dissolve cornstarch in water.

Add to sauce to thicken.

Sprinkle with peppercorns.

Drizzle over freshwater tilapia in a parsley-crumb coat (recipe above).

Jasmine Rice

Ingredients (6 servings)

3 tablespoons extra-virgin olive oil

2 bay leaves

2½ cups jasmine rice

5 cups water

salt

Instructions

Warm oil in large saucepan on medium-low heat.

Add bay leaves and rice.

Stir until rice is well coated.

Add water and salt to taste.

Raise heat to medium.

Bring to a fast simmer.

Lower heat to a light simmer.

Cook until water is absorbed.

Cover and remove from heat.

Let stand 40 minutes.

Serve with freshwater tilapia in a parsley-crumb coat (recipe above).

Variety of Stir Fried Vegetables

Ingredients (6 servings)

¾ cup onions, sliced

¼ cup green Bell peppers, sliced

¼ cup red Bell peppers, sliced

¼ cup yellow Bell peppers, sliced

¾ cup mushrooms, sliced

3 teaspoons extra-virgin olive oil

salt

fresh ground black pepper

1 half fresh lime

Instructions

Heat oil in skillet on medium heat.

Stir in vegetables.

Season to taste with salt and pepper.

Cover and cook 2 minutes.

Remove from heat.

Squeeze the juice from half a fresh lime over vegetables.

Serve hot with freshwater tilapia in a parsley-crumb coat (recipe above).

Sea Scallops Mediterranean Fashion

Sea Scallops

Ingredients (6 Servings)

1½ pound sea scallops

1½ tablespoons extra-virgin olive oil

Instructions

Heat olive oil in large skillet on medium-high heat.

Add scallops.

Sauté 8 minutes.

Scallops are done when opaque.

Serve on bed of eggplant, tomatoes, zucchini, black olives, capers and fresh herbs (recipe below).

Bed Of Eggplant, Tomatoes, Zucchini, Black Olives, Capers And Fresh Herbs

Ingredients (6 servings)

1 tablespoon extra-virgin olive oil

1 pound eggplant, cubed

¾ cup zucchini, cubed

¼ cup celery, chopped

¼ cup onion, chopped

3 garlic cloves, minced

1 pound roma tomatoes, cubed

½ cup parsley, chopped fine

¼ cup yellow raisins

¼ cup black olives, pitted and coarsely chopped

½ tablespoon light brown sugar

½ teaspoon capers, coarsely chopped

½ teaspoon salt

¼ teaspoon fresh ground black pepper

2 teaspoons balsamic vinegar

Instructions

Heat olive oil in Dutch oven on medium-high heat.

Add eggplant, zucchini, celery, onion and garlic.

Sauté 10 minutes.

Add tomatoes, pardley, raisins, olives, sugar, capers, salt and pepper.

Bring to a boil.

Cover and lower heat to a simmer.

Cook 15 minutes, stirring intermittently.

Remove cover and cook until liquid mostly evaporates.

Stir in balsamic vinegar.

Serve warm with sea scallops (recipe above).

Young Tom Turkey and All the Trimmings

Young Tom Turkey with Dried Fruit Stuffing and Giblet Gravy

Ingredients (6 Servings)

1 young tom turkey (12 pounds).

1 pound Hawaiian sweet bread, cubed 1"

½ cup mixed raisins

¼ cup dried cherries

¼ cup dried cranberries

¼ cup currants

¼ cup celery, diced

½ cup honey mead

salt

fresh ground black pepper

¾ cup unsalted butter

10 tablespoons all-purpose flour

2 teaspoons water

3 cups turkey broth

1 turkey heart

1 turkey gizzard

1 hard-boiled egg, chopped fine

Instructions

Cut wing tips from turkey. (Can be used for broth or soup.)

Season turkey inside and out with salt and pepper to taste.

Put bread cubes, raisins, dried fruit, currants, celery and mead in large bowl.

Mix stuffing well.

Fill turkey cavity with stuffing

Flex thigh and wing joints and truss turkey with string.

Mix 4 tablespoons butter with 4 tablespoons flour.

Rub turkey all over with butter-flour mixture. Massage in thoroughly.

Sprinkle remaining flour in the bottom of roasting pan.

Place roasting rack inside pan.

Position turkey breast-up on rack.

Let sit 30 minutes.

Preheat oven to 450°F.

Place roasting pan in oven.

Roast 45 minutes.

While turkey cooks, melt remaining butter in small saucepan.

Add water and stir well.

Baste turkey with melted butter mix.

Lower heat to 350°F.

Roast 1 hour 40 minutes. Baste frequently with melted butter mix.

Remove turkey from oven. Let stand 20 minutes.

Transfer to carving board.

Bring turkey broth to boil in saucepan.

Add turkey heart and gizzard.

Lower heat to simmer.

Cook 10 minutes.

Strain. Reserve and set aside broth.

Chop giblets fine. Set aside.

While turkey stands, skim off semi-transparent liquid from roast pan drippings.

Place unwashed roast pan on stove top.

Add reserved broth.

Scrape pan until browned particles on bottom and sides of pan dissolve.

Strain broth into saucepan.

Bring to boil.

Lower heat to simmer.

Cook 10 minutes. Skim surface as needed.

Add chopped giblets and egg.

Carve turkey and serve with gravy on the side. Serve with cranberry sauce (recipe below), corn pudding (recipe below) and glazed sweet potatoes (recipe below).

Cranberry Sauce

Ingredients (6 servings)

4 cups fresh cranberries

1 cup orange juice

1 cup sugar

Instructions

Combine orange juice and ½ cup sugar in saucepan.

Bring to a simmer on medium-low heat.

Add cranberries, stir and bring to boil.

Return heat to simmer.

Cook 15 minutes. Stir intermittently.

Sauce is done when berries have popped.

Remove from heat.

Sweeten to taste with remaining sugar.

Let stand 15 minutes.

Serve with young tom turkey with dried fruit stuffing and giblet gravy (recipe above).

Corn Pudding

Ingredients (6 servings)

¼ cup sugar

3 tablespoons all-purpose flour

2 teaspoons baking powder

1½ teaspoons salt

6 eggs

2 cups heavy cream

½ cup melted butter

6 cups fresh corn kernels

Instructions

Preheat oven to 350°F.

Combine sugar, flour, baking powder and salt in bowl.

Whisk eggs, cream, and butter in separate bowl.

Slowly add sugar mixture.

Whisk smooth.

Add corn. Stir well.

Pour mixture into buttered baking dish.

Bake 50 minutes.

Pudding is done when set and golden brown.

Let stand 5 minutes.

Serve with young tom turkey with dried fruit stuffing and giblet gravy (recipe above).

Glazed Sweet Potatoes

Ingredients (6 servings)

3 sweet potatoes

¼ cup maple syrup

2 tablespoons brown sugar

Instructions

Put sweet potatoes in large saucepan.

Cover with water.

Bring to boil.

Lower heat to simmer.

Cover and cook 30 minutes.

Sweet potatoes are done when tender. Let stand to cool.

Preheat oven to 350°F.

Butter an 8"x8" roasting pan.

Peel cooled sweet potatoes.

Cut into large chunks.

Arrange chunks in buttered roasting pan.

Melt butter, syrup and sugar together in small saucepan on low heat.

Cook 5 minutes. Stir continuously.

Drizzle mixture over sweet potato chunks.

Place in oven.

Bake 7 minutes.

Sweet potatoes are done when tops are glazed and light brown.

Serve hot with young tom turkey with dried fruit stuffing and giblet gravy (recipe above).

Prime Rib of Beef au Jus

Prime Rib of Beef au Jus

Ingredients (6 Servings)

5½ lb bone-in prime rib

6 cloves garlic, cut into thin slivers

salt

fresh ground black pepper

2 cups dry red wine

4 cups beef stock

1 tablespoon fresh thyme, chopped

2 teaspoons fresh rosemary, chopped

Instructions

Preheat oven to 450°F.

Cut shallow slits all over prime rib with tip of sharp knife.

Fill each slit with a sliver of garlic.

Season generously salt and pepper.

Place roast, bones down on roasting rack set inside roasting pan.

Insert meat thermometer in centre of roast. Avoid fat or bone.

Oven sear 10 minutes in 450°F oven.

Reduce heat to 350°F.

Roast 2 hours until thermometer reads 140°F for medium-rare. (Roast 2½ hours until thermometer reads 155°F for medium).

Remove roast from oven and transfer to cutting board.

Cover with foil to keep warm.

Place roasting pan of drippings over 2 burners on high heat.

Add wine.

Cook to a reduction on high heat, stirring pan bottom with wooden spoon.

Add beef stock.

Cook until au ju reduces in half.

Whisk in thyme and rosemary.

Season to taste with salt and pepper.

Carve roast into thin slices.

Serve beef with au jus sauce, grilled tomato (recipe follows), corn-on-the-cob (recipe follows) and brioche potato (recipe follows).

Grilled Tomato

Ingredients (6 Servings)

6 beefsteak tomatoes, halved

1 teaspoon parsley, chopped fine

salt

fresh ground black pepper

Instructions

Preheat grill on high.

Season tomatoes to taste with salt and pepper.

Cook 10 minutes under grill.

Sprinkle parsley over tomatoes.

Serve with Prime Rib of Beef au Jus (recipe above).

Corn-On-The-Cob

Ingredients (6 Servings)

6 ears fresh corn

2 tablespoons butter

2 teaspoons lemon juice

1 teaspoon fresh thyme, chopped fine

Instructions

Peel corn husks back

Remove silk from corn.

Pull husks back around corn.

Place in large pot.

Cover with cold water.

Let soak 1 hour.

Drain. Shake out excess water.

Check corn is covered by husks. Tie tips together with wet kitchen string if needed.

Preheat grill on medium-high.

Grill corn 25 minutes. Turn intermittently.

Corn is done when tender.

Remove husks and string.

Combine butter, lemon juice and thyme in small saucepan.

Heat on medium-high until butter melts.

Brush melted butter mix over corn.

Serve hot with Prime Rib of Beef au Jus (recipe above).

Brioche Potato

Ingredients (6 Servings)

4 pounds boiled potatoes, riced

3 egg yolks

4 tablespoons butter

egg wash (1 tablespoon milk mixed with 1 egg yolk)

salt

fresh ground black pepper

Instructions

Preheat oven to 450°F.

Mix all ingredients well in large bowl.

Let stand 30 minutes.

Butter 6 brioche molds.

Sprinkle a clean work surface with flour.

Scoop 1/3 cup potato mix into a ball.

Roll potato ball in flour.

Place in potato ball in brioche mold.

Cut a notch in the top of the potato.

Make a smaller ball rolled in flour and put on top of the first ball.

Repeat process to fill all 6 brioche molds.

Brush egg wash lightly over each brioche.

Bake 30 minutes.

Brioche is done when tops are golden brown.

Remove from molds.

Serve hot with Prime Rib of Beef au Jus (recipe above).

The Princess Love Boat Dream

Ingredients (6 Servings)

1 pound bittersweet chocolate

8 ounces unsalted butter

6 egg yolks

8 egg whites

3 ounces Lady Godiva chocolate liqueur

½ cup caster sugar

3 tablespoons vanilla flavored sugar

16 fresh mint leaves

¼ cup white chocolate, grated.

¼ cup milk chocolate, grated.

2 tablespoons bittersweet cocoa

Instructions

Melt bittersweet chocolate in double boiler.

Remove from heat.

Add butter. Mix smooth.

Blend in egg yolks and Godiva liqueur.

Whisk egg whites to very stiff peaks.

Add the caster sugar and vanilla flavored sugar

Gradually fold egg white mix into chocolate mix.

Pour into heart shaped mold.

Refrigerate 12 hours.

Remove from mold to serving platter.

Unmold the chocolate and place in the center of the plate.

Garnish with grated white and milk chocolate.

Dust with cocoa powder.

Garnish mousse with mint leaves.

Serve chilled.

Fresh Fruit Gratin

Ingredients (6 Servings)

2 pounds fresh mixed fruit (strawberries, raspberries, blackberries, red currants and blueberries)

3 fresh peaches

2 cups crumbled amaretti

8 tablespoons fresh squeezed orange juice

zest of 1 lemon,

2 egg whites

2 tablespoons caster sugar

½ teaspoon vanilla extract

2 egg yolks

½ cup honey

1 cup dry white wine

¾ cup low-fat yogurt

6 mint leaves

Instructions

Rinse fruits.

Remove peach pits.

Chop peaches into bite size chunks.

Put fruit in baking dish.

Crumble amaretti. Sprinkle over fruit.

Mix orange juice and lemon zest.

Sprinkle zest mix on top.

Let sit 30 minutes.

Preheat oven to 375°F.

Whisk egg whites to stiff peaks in medium bowl.

Slowly mix in sugar and vanilla.

Whisk to a gloss.

Spread the egg whites over fruit and crumbs.

Sculpt as desired.

Bake 10 minutes.

Remove fruit gratin from oven and set aside.

Whisk egg yolks and honey 3 minutes in double boiler.

Add wine when light colored and thickened.

Continuously whisk to soft peaks.

When light and fluffy, float double boiler bowl in large bowl of ice water.

Let zabaglione cool.

Fold yogurt in.

Serve fruit gratin with spoonful of zabaglione.

Garnish each serving with a mint leaf.

Brandy Alexander Pie

Ingredients (6 Servings)

1½ cups graham cracker crumbs, crushed very fine

1/3 cup sugar

6 tablespoons melted butter

2 leaves white gelatin

2 cups heavy cream

3 egg yolks

¼ cup caster sugar

½ teaspoon vanilla extract

1 tablespoon cognac

½ cup Cocoa Krispies® for garnish

Instructions

Preheat oven to 375°F.

Combine cracker crumbs, sugar and melted butter in bowl.

Mix well.

Press mixture into pie mold.

Bake 10 minutes.

Remove from oven and set aside to cool.

Soak gelatin in cold water to soften.

Whisk cream to stiff peaks in mixing bowl.

Combine egg yolks, vanilla and caster sugar in bowl.

Whisk until pale and creamy.

Warm the cognac in small saucepan on medium heat.

Remove when hot.

Squeeze excess water out of gelatin leaves.

Dissolve gelatin in hot cognac.

Add cognac to egg yolk mixture. Stir well.

Whisk one third of the whipped cream into the egg yolk mixture.

Gently fold one third of the whipped cream in.

Pour egg-cream into graham cracker crust.

Cover and refrigerate 1 hour.

Top with remaining whipped cream and garnish with chocolate rice crispies.

CHAPTER EIGHT

Dessert – Extras, Helpful Hints & Cruise Contact Info.

We hope you enjoyed your fantasy cruise as much as we enjoyed creating it. We strived to give you a taste of not only the amazing food but also the cruise ship experience. A good cruise on a good line is a truly memorable event. We've done our best to bring you scaled down versions of each and every item on the menus we selected. A little repetition was unavoidable in order to include the widest variety of amazing culinary delights. Cooking for an intimate few is of course different than cooking for thousands of diners but we truly hope we succeeded in replicating the dishes as closely as possible. Any errors or omissions are our own and we welcome your feedback should you discover one.

We would like to thank all the wonderfully helpful cruise line staff that aided in the compilation of menus and recipes presented in this book. Without you this book would not be possible. A special thank you to Holland America who sent us the following delicious recipes from their **HOLLAND AMERICA LINE GOES WILD FOR ALASKAN SALMON** menus that are simply too good to leave out even though they weren't on the menu we chose to include.

Grilled Salmon with Ginger-Cilantro Pesto on Sautéed Watercress

Serve with basmati rice. — Yield: 4 servings

Ingredients

1 cup chopped fresh cilantro

½ cup chopped green onions

1/3 cup salted roasted macadamia nuts

¼ cup chopped peeled fresh ginger

¼ teaspoon cayenne pepper

7 tablespoons vegetable oil

Salt and freshly ground black pepper to taste

4 6-ounce pieces salmon fillet

1 large garlic clove, minced

2 tablespoons olive oil

3 bunches of watercress, coarse stems discarded and the watercress rinsed but not spun dry

Instructions

Combine first 5 ingredients in food processor. Blend until nuts are finely chopped. Add 6 tablespoons oil and process until well blended. Season to taste with salt and pepper. (Can be made 1 day ahead. Cover; chill. Bring to room temperature before using.)

Prepare grill.

Brush salmon with remaining 1 tablespoon vegetable oil and sprinkle with salt and pepper to taste. Grill salmon on an oiled rack set 5 to 6 inches over glowing coals until just cooked through, about 5 minutes on each side.

Meanwhile, in a large heavy skillet sauté the garlic in the olive oil over moderately high heat for 30 seconds, or until it is fragrant. Add the watercress, and stir the mixture until it is combined well. Sauté the watercress, covered, for 2 to 3 minutes, or until it is just wilted, and Season to taste with salt and pepper.

To serve, put sautéed watercress in the center of 4 plates. Top with the salmon and spoon pesto around. Serve basmati rice alongside.

Cedar-Planked Salmon in an Asian-Style Marinade with Pickled Ginger and Watercress Salad — HEART HEALTHY RECIPE

Alternative: Salmon can just be grilled directly instead of plank. — Yield: 6 servings

Ingredients

Salmon

1 cedar grilling plank (15 x 6 ½ x 3/8-inch)

½ cup rice vinegar

½ cup low-sodium soy sauce

2 tablespoons honey

1 teaspoon ground ginger

½ teaspoon freshly ground black pepper

3 garlic cloves, minced

1 lemon, thinly sliced

1 3 ½ -pound salmon fillet

¼ cup chopped scallions

1 tablespoon sesame seeds, toasted

Instructions

Immerse and soak the plank in water 1 hour; drain.

To prepare grill for indirect grilling, heat one side of the grill to high heat.

Combine vinegar and the next 6 ingredients (vinegar through lemon) in a large zip-top plastic bag; seal. Shake to combine. Add fish; seal. Marinate in refrigerator 30 minutes, turning once.

Place plank on grill rack over high heat; grill 5 minutes or until lightly charred. Carefully turn plank over; move to cool side of grill. Remove fish from marinade; discard marinade. Place fish, skin side down, on charred side of plank. Cover and grill 15 minutes or until fish flakes easily when tested with a fork.

To serve, place on bed of Pickled Ginger and Watercress Salad (recipe follows) on 6 plates. Top with portions of salmon and sprinkle with scallions and sesame seeds.

Pickled Ginger and Watercress Salad

Ingredients

1 clove garlic, crushed

1/8 teaspoon kosher salt

1 tablespoon liquid from a jar of picked ginger

1 tablespoon fresh lime juice or rice wine vinegar

1 tablespoon canola oil

1 teaspoon honey

Freshly ground black pepper to taste

6 cups stemmed, washed and dried watercress

4 scallions, chopped

1/3cup drained pickled ginger

Instructions

With the side of a chef's knife, mash garlic with salt. Place in a small bowl or a jar with a tight-fitting lid. Add ginger liquid, lime juice (or vinegar), oil, honey and pepper; whisk or shake until blended.

Place watercress, scallions and pickled ginger in a large bowl. Just before serving, toss with dressing.

Salmon Baked in Phyllo with Shiitake Mushrooms and Champagne Sauce

Serve with roasted asparagus. — Yield: 4 servings

Ingredients

½ cup uncooked brown basmati rice

2 sticks (8 ounces) unsalted butter

½ pound fresh shiitake mushrooms, stems removed, caps cut into ¼-inch dice

3 large shallots, minced

1 teaspoon fresh lemon juice

1 tablespoon chopped fresh dill

¾ teaspoon salt

1/8 teaspoon freshly ground black pepper

8 sheets phyllo dough

4 salmon fillets (each about 6 ounces), skin removed

¼ cup dry white wine or Champagne

2 tablespoons white wine vinegar

Instructions

In a small saucepan, bring 1 ½ cups water to a boil. Add the rice, cover and cook over low heat until tender but still a bit chewy, about 30 to 45 minutes. Add up to ¼ cup more water if needed. Drain the rice in a colander and set aside.

In a large skillet, melt 2 tablespoons of the butter over high heat. When the foam subsides, add the mushrooms and 2/3 of the shallots. Cook, stirring frequently, until the shallots are soft and the mushrooms are lightly browned, about 5 minutes. Transfer to a medium bowl and toss with 1 tablespoon butter. Stir well to coat and then add the cooked rice, lemon juice, 2 teaspoons of the dill, ½ teaspoon salt and the pepper. Set aside. Cut 1 stick plus 2 tablespoons of the butter into 1-inch pieces and refrigerate.

In a small saucepan, melt the remaining 3 tablespoons butter over low heat. Cut the sheets of phyllo in half crosswise to 12-by-8-inch rectangles. Place one piece of phyllo on a work surface; keep the rest covered with a damp towel as you work. Brush the sheet lightly with the melted butter. Place other sheet of phyllo on top, butter it and repeat until you have 4 stacked sheets of buttered phyllo. Place a piece of salmon diagonally in the center. Top with ½ cup of the rice mixture.

To form the package, bring the corners of the phyllo dough up over the salmon to meet in the center. Gather the pastry and fold the corner tips back slightly. Separate the layers of phyllo to make a petal effect on top. Repeat with the remaining phyllo, melted butter, salmon and rice. Place the salmon packages on a baking sheet and refrigerate for at least 20 minutes and up to 4 hours.

Preheat the oven to 350°F.. Bake the salmon packages in the upper third of the oven for about 25 minutes, until the phyllo is brown and crisp on top and an instant-reading thermometer inserted into the fish registers 140 degrees F.

Meanwhile, in a small nonreactive saucepan, combine the wine, vinegar and the remaining shallots and boil over high heat until reduced to 1 tablespoon, about 7 minutes. Remove from the heat and whisk in the chilled butter pieces, several at a time, adding more when the butter is nearly melted. Continue whisking until all the butter has been added and the sauce is thick. Strain the sauce through a fine sieve into another saucepan and add the remaining 1 teaspoon dill, ¼ teaspoon salt, and a pinch of pepper. Set aside. Just before serving, whisk the sauce over moderate heat until just warm.

To serve, place each salmon package on a warmed dinner plate. Cut the packages in half and open slightly. Pour the sauce between the package halves and around the salmon.

*   *   *

Several recipes in this book make use of puff pastry. We include the following recipe for creating puff pastry dough for use in those recipes.

Puff Pastry

Ingredients

3 cups unbleached all-purpose flour

1 cup plain bleached cake flour

6½ sticks unsalted butter, chilled

1½ teaspoons salt

1 cup ice water

Instructions

Dice butter sticks into ½ -inch cubes.

Put flour in mixing bowl.

Add butter and salt.

Blend flour and butter together until butter broken into small lumps.

Blend in water and mix until dough clumps roughly together but butter pieces remain the same.

On a lightly floured work surface, quickly push, pat and roll dough to form a 12-inch by 18-inch rectangle.

Lightly flour top of dough.

Using a pastry sheet, flip the bottom of the rectangle up over the middle.

Flip the top of the rectangle down to cover it.

Lift the dough away from the work surface using a pastry sheet.

Clean the work surface and lightly.

Return the dough to the work surface. Set it with the top flap to your right.

Lightly flour top of the dough, and push, pat and roll again into a rectangle.

Repeat folding as above. (Each "roll-and-fold" operation is called a "turn".

Repeat process 2 more times. (4 "turns" in total).

After the last "turn" you will see flakes of butter scattered below the surface on the dough.

Wrap dough in plastic wrap and place in a plastic bag.

Refrigerate 40 minutes.

Repeat "turn" process 2 more times.

Let dough rest 30 minutes.

Dough is ready for baking when rubbery and difficult to roll.

*   *   *

Lobster Hints - Know how many guests you are cooking for. Purchase one 6-8 ounce lobster tail for each guest. Cold-water varieties are best. Lobster tails from Maine, Australia, New Zealand or South Africa are ideal for baking. The meat is whiter and sweeter. When purchasing warm-water lobster tails, check for black spots on the meat. Choose tails that are spot-free with white, not gray. Lobster tails are also available frozen. While fresh is best, frozen is a viable alternative with proper thawing. Thaw lobster tails in the refrigerator a day before you bake them. Keep them as cold as possible prior to cooking. Trying to speed up the thawing process risk accelerated growth of bacteria.

* * *

Prime Rib Hints - Let the roast stand a minimum of 15 minutes before carving. Use a gentle sawing action and a sharp knife to minimize loss of juices while carving. Set the cutting board on a rimmed baking sheet to collect juices. With a fork, position roast so bones are vertical. Carve along bones to remove meat. Set deboned meat rib side down. Cut crossgrain into thin slices. To serve the rib bones, simply cut between bones and separate them. For supreme ease of carving, ask your butcher when buying to cut meat from the bones and tie them back on. After roasting, cut the twine, remove bones and carve.

* * *

Baked Potatoes Hints –Be sure skin is an even brown tone with no green tinge. Inspect thoroughly for bruises, discolored spots and sprouts. Sprouts can be toxic but it takes a lot of them to make you ill. Do not buy potatoes that have sprouted or are tinted green. Potatoes with a green tinge were exposed to too much light. A natural reaction in the potato to too much light increases Solanine content. The chemical Solanine, when eaten in quantity, can cause sickness. Most of the vitamins and minerals in potatoes are in the skins. and you can eat the skins of perfect potatoes. Clean them but do not soak the potatoes as it makes them soggy. Do not use hot water or outside will start to cook and the inside won't catch up. When baking a lot of potatoes at once, select potatoes of similar shape and size. They will cook more evenly and be done at the same time. Wrapping in aluminum foil produces a soft non-crispy skin. This steams rather than bakes so the light, flaky texture of baking will be missing. The texture of a steamed potato is completely different from that of a baked potato. Do not use aluminum foil when baking potatoes. The higher the oven temperature, the briefer the cooking time and the crisper the skin. Large take longer to bake. Bake potatoes along with your other baking. Judge cooking time by oven temperature, 45 minutes at 400°F., 60 minutes at 350°F. and 90 minutes at 325°F.

*   *   *

Cruise Line Contact Information

Celebrity Cruises
www.celebritycruises.com
1-888-276-2874

Crystal Cruises
www.crystalcruise.com
1-800-337-9568

Cunard
www.cunard.com
1-800-728-6273

Holland America Line
www.hollandamerica.com
1-877-932-4259

MSC Cruises
www.msccruises.com
1-877-665-4655

Norwegian Cruise Line (NCL)
www.ncl.com
1-866-234-7350

Princess Cruises
www.princess.com
1-800-774-6237

Royal Caribbean International
www.royalcaribbean.com
(866) 562-7625

If you have any questions about any of the menus, please contact the author at:
Diana@dianarubino.com

INDEX

Broiled Lobster Tail served with a frothy Tarragon and Shallot Butter, 276
Broiled Marinated Lobster, 150
Broiled Marinated Lobster and Rice Creole, 150
Brown Sauce Enhanced With Pink Peppercorn, 398
Bucatini with Duck Confit, 279
Bucatini with Duck Confit served boneless over Pasta with sautéed Mushrooms
*   and diced Zucchini enhanced with a delicate Sauce, 279*
Butter Pecan and Vanilla Ice Cream with Chocolate Frozen Yogurt, Mint Sauce, 80
Buttered Croutons, 142

C

Caesar Salad, 319
Caesar with Tossed Romaine Lettuce, Parmesan Cheese and Croutons, 265
California Rosé Wine-Shallots Sauce, 220
Calvados-Spiked Forest Mushroom Ragoût, 350
Caper Pâté, 132
Caramelized Pear Napoleon, 297
Caramelized Pears, 297
Cardinale, 113
Carmelized Pears and Strawberries, 72
Cedar-Planked Salmon, 427
Cedar-Planked Salmon in an Asian-Style Marinade with Pickled Ginger and
*   Watercress Salad, 427*
Celebrity, 246
Celebrity Cruises, 438
Cesare Ensalata, 96
Champagne and Saffron Sauce, 213
Champagne Vinaigrette Dressing, 392
Chantilly cream, 245
Cheese Fondue, 159
Cheese Fondue Sauce, 192
Cheese Selection with Munster, Brie, Stilton, Gloucester, 81
Cherry Compote, 76
Cherry Tomatoes & Pine Nuts, 24
Cherry Tomatoes and Pine Nuts, 28
Chicken Consommé, 40
Chicken Consommé & Matzo Balls, 40
Chicory & Flaked Blue Cheese, 44
Chicory & Flaked Blue Cheese, Apple Sherry Dressing, 44
Chilled Berry and Cumin Yogurt, 263
Chilled Cantaloupe Melon Tartar, Citrus & Mint Marmalade, Basil Jell, 32
Chilled Curried Pumpkin and Williams Pear Cream Soup, 387
Chipolata Sausage, 58
Chipolata Stuffing, 56

D

E

F

G

H

N

O

P

Petite Marmite "Henry IV", 261
Petits Pains au Chocolat, 173
Philadelphia Pepper Pot, 382
Pickled Ginger and Watercress Salad, 429
Pineapple with Alaskan Berries, 309
Pink Cream Sauce, 147
Pinzimonio, 90
Plum Torte, 243
Poached Sea Bass, 211
Pojarsky vegetables, 157
Pojarsky Vegetables Served with Cheese Fondue, 157
Porcini Mushroom Broth, 94
Potatoes Croquettes, 160
President Carter's Sautéed Supreme of Chicken with Dry Sack Sherry with Red
and Green Peppers and Tomato Rice Pilaf, 214
President Ford's Plum Torte Chantilly, 243
President Ford's Smoked Norwegian Salmon Terrine with Red Salmon Caviar
Sauce, 184
President Johnson's Chocolate Mousse with Toasted Hazelnuts-and-Brandy
Sauce, 239
President Johnson's Grilled Butterflied Tenderloin of Beef with Crimini
Mushrooms served with Honey Glazed Baby Carrots and New, 225
President Nixon's North Atlantic Crab Soup with French Bread Croutons, 197
President Reagan's Gruyère Cheese Crepes Fondue, 190
President Reagan's Floating Island with Cointreau Sauce, 236
President Reagan's Roast Rack of Lamb, California Rosé Wine-Shallots Sauce,
Princess Potatoes and Fennel Gratinée, 218
Pressed & Seared Tofu on Red Lentil Curry, 66
Prime Rib Hints, 436
Prime Rib of Beef – the finest cut of Roast Beef presented with Baked Potato,
Natural Juice and Creamed Horseradish, 287
Prime Rib of Beef au Jus, 287, 411
Princess Cruises, 438
Princess Potatoes, 221
prosciutto crudo, 126
Puff Pastry, 434
Puff Pastry Toast, 135

Q

Queen Mary 2, 9

R

Radicchio Salad & Blood Oranges, 43
Red Bell Pepper Dressing, 209
Red Salmon Caviar Sauce, 186
Regal Princess, 368
Rice Creole, 151
Ricotta Cake, 65
Risotto with Green Apple and Champagne, 148
Roast Capon, 54
Roast Capon, Chipolata Stuffing & Sage Gravy, 54
Roast Rack of Lamb, 218
Roasted Artichokes, 24, 27
Roasted Red Pepper Salad, 92
Roasted Vegetables, 51
Rosemary Vinaigrette, 22
Roses of Norwegian Salmon, 128
Roses of Norwegian Salmon, with Rustic Salad and Croutons with Caper Pâté,
   128
Rossini, 115
Royal Caribbean, 84
Royal Caribbean International, 438
Rustic Salad, 129

S

Sage Gravy, 60
Salmon Baked in Phyllo with Shiitake Mushrooms and Champagne Sauce, 430
Saltimbocca Alla Romano, 100
Sautéed Mushrooms and diced Zucchini, 283
Sautéed Shrimps ", 330
Sautéed Shrimps with Garlic, 330
Sautéed Supreme of Chicken with Dry Sack Sherry with Red and Green Peppers,
   214
Sea Scallops, 401
Sea Scallops Mediterranean Fashion, 401
Selected Fruit with a Rum and Coconut Sauce, 253
Sesame Seed Twist, 202
Sevruga Caviar with Classical Garnish, 31
Shrimp Bisque, 37, 321
Shrimp Bisque with Corn Custard, Baby Shrimp, 37
Shrimp Bisque with Sourdough Croutons, 321
Shrimp Cocktail, 254
Slow Braised Short Ribs, 336

Small Assorted Pastries, 167
Smoked Norwegian Salmon Terrine, 184
Sourdough Croutons, 323
Spanish Salad, 162
Spinach and Pear Salad, 22
Spinach Lasagna, 230
Steamed Black Mussels, Saffron Veloute, 35
Steamed Potatoes, 274
Steamed Potatoes & Seasonal Vegetables, 109
Sticky Rice, 334
Stir Fried Vegetables, 400
Stuffed Eggplant, 24
Stuffed Eggplants, 24
Sugar Free Strawberry Mousse, 77
Sugar Free Strawberry Mousse with Fresh Berry Salad, 77
Summit, 246
Sun-Dried Tomato Risotto, 353
Supreme of Chicken Terrine, 256

T

Tarragon Sauce, 137
Tarragon Shallot Butter, 278
The Master Chef "Premiere", 364
Tiramisu, 110
Toasted Hazelnuts, 242
Tomato Concassé, 332
Tomato Rice Pilaf, 216
Tropical Ice Cream Cup - Vanilla Ice cream with Rum, Coconut, Raisins and
    Whipped Cream, 175
Turkey with Dried Fruit Stuffing and Giblet Gravy, 404

V,W

Vanilla Rum Creme Anglaise, 363
Warm Montrachet Cheese and Potato Gratin, 258
Veal Cordon Bleu stuffed with Country Smoked Ham and Emmenthal Cheese,
    lightly coated with White Bread Crumbs, shallow fried un, 284
Vegetable Strudel, 356
Vegetable Strudel With Chive and Mushroom Sauce and Golden Rissole Potatoes,
    356
William Potato, 346
Vol-au-Vent a la Reine, 379

Y

Z

END

Made in the USA
Middletown, DE
22 August 2019